Public Pensions and City Solvency

THE CITY IN THE TWENTY-FIRST CENTURY

Eugenie L. Birch and Susan M. Wachter, Series Editors

A complete list of books in the series is available from the publisher.

Public Pensions and City Solvency

Edited by Susan M. Wachter

PENN

University of Pennsylvania Press
Philadelphia

Published by
University of Pennsylvania Press
Philadelphia, Pennsylvania 19104-4112
www.upenn.edu/pennpress

Printed in the United States of America

A Cataloging-in-Publication record is available from the
Library of Congress

Cover design by John Hubbard

ISBN 978-0-8122-4826-5 hardcover
ISBN 978-0-8122-9287-9 ebook

Contents

Preface

Susan M. Wachter

In October 1975, with New York City on the brink of bankruptcy, Mayor Abraham D. Beame asked the federal government for help. The answer came back in the negative. In a headline the next day, the *New York Daily News* proclaimed, "Ford to City: Drop Dead." And it nearly did. But crisis was averted in the days that followed. Mayor Beame met with all the major creditors and union leaders, and everyone agreed to take the necessary cuts to make the debt payments and return the city to solvency, showing that this is possible. While cities have as a group strengthened their economies and fortunes considerably since then, there is one area where weakness is still a major concern: the preparation for paying promised pension liabilities.

In this volume you will find the best estimates of the pension liabilities of large U.S. cities. Since the end of the Great Recession, as this volume demonstrates, despite a booming stock market, the underfunding problem has worsened in these cities. Citizens and all claimants to pensions are ultimately at risk. This volume explains this risk, which ultimately can be reversed by more attention, information, and transparency. In the absence of good information, leaders are not rewarded for good decisions; rather, the lack of attention and information protects those officials who ride to victory on the backs of shortsighted policies. It is time to peel back the veil.

In cities facing future financial crises, there are a multitude of challenges today: city budgets are under financial strain, globalization is siphoning off stable middle-class jobs, and an aging population has pushed the retiree-to-worker ratio to new heights. Public services cost money, and there is no magic wand to make that equation disappear. Nonetheless, the long-run challenges need to be addressed as well. Attention must be paid to the need for a new balance between taxes and spending that is sustainable.

The longer cities delay this rebalancing, the more likely the fiscal burden will veer out of control. The goal of this volume is to point to this need, even as cities revitalize across America. Citizens ultimately must demand accountability, but they cannot do so until the problem is brought into the light. This book focuses a beacon squarely where it belongs, but it is only the beginning. The challenge remains for those who read it to carry our cities forward into a brighter, more transparent, more fiscally responsible future.

I would like to thank Cara Griffin, Scott Mactas, and Anthony Orlando, who provided invaluable research and editorial assistance in the development of this book.

Public Pensions and City Solvency

Foreword

Richard Ravitch

Cities and states in America are facing fiscal stress in historic proportions. There is relatively limited public understanding of the severity of these circumstances. One of the reasons that there is not greater awareness is the failure of our educational system to address these problems in a serious way. There are exceptions, the most notable of which is the Wharton School and many of its faculty members; Robert Inman and Susan Wachter are among those who address this issue in their teaching and their writing, as do the other exemplary authors included in this insightful and important volume.

Just over fifty years ago, two extraordinary changes were taking place in most urban jurisdictions around the country: public employees secured the right to collectively bargain for their wages and benefits, and the United States embarked on a series of efforts to expand services in order to address the problems of poverty, discrimination, and inadequate health care. The values implicit in a commitment to social justice dominated our politics and the result was a vast increase in government spending. Federal grants were inevitably accompanied by requirements that state and local governments match some percentage of what the feds were appropriating. The primary example is Medicaid, which requires in essence a 50 percent match.

These programs were popular and, during a period of significant economic growth, public employment at the state and local levels expanded to provide these services, and the compensation of those public employees grew as well. When we had a recession in the mid-1970s and our politics became more conservative, politicians were increasingly unwilling to impose more taxes to increase current compensation for the people who worked for them. What they were willing to do, however, was to increase health care and retirement benefits that didn't have to be funded currently and therefore had no impact on the budget in the year they were promised.

The costs of meeting these obligations have continued to grow much faster than the economy. Low interest rates, declining public employment, and increasing longevity have all contributed to the underfunding of our public pension funds. But if that itself wasn't sufficient to sound alarm bells, politicians around the country have often failed to make the actuarially required contribution to these plans and to adequately fund their health care obligations. There are thus trillions of dollars of underfunding of promises that were made in good faith, all of which are contractually obligated and some of which are constitutionally obligated.

States and local governments have responded to these circumstances in many ways. Unfortunately, many have addressed budget deficits by using the proceeds of borrowing or the proceeds of asset sales to meet cash requirements. These are unsustainable ways of dealing with the underlying problem. We are now seeing dramatic underfunding of minimal infrastructure and educational needs, litigation over the enforceability of these promises, and, increasingly, bankruptcy filings by those governments that have the statutory authority to do so.

Perhaps of even greater significance is the fact that the federal government is reducing domestic discretionary spending, which will have an even more alarming impact on the ability of states and cities to meet their obligations, both social and contractual. There is $650 billion in the federal discretionary budget pass-throughs to state and local governments. A 10 percent cut, which is realistically possible, would have a devastating impact on the capacity of local governments to meet their obligations.

This book will hopefully help the voters elect public officials who deal with these issues responsibly so that our grandchildren are not burdened with the obligation to pay for the benefits our generation has been so fortunate to have enjoyed.

1 Why City Pension Problems Have Not Improved, and a Roadmap Forward

Joshua D. Rauh

In the aftermath of the 2009 financial crisis, large unfunded pension liabilities emerged in the reported accounts of U.S. state and local governments. Studies by the Pew Charitable Trust, among other sources, estimated that the unfunded liabilities were around $1 trillion at the state level and around $100 billion at the city level (Pew Center on the States 2010, 2013). Using default-free discounting procedures consistent with the principles of financial economics, and relying on market values (as opposed to smoothed actuarial value) of assets, Novy-Marx and Rauh (2011b, 2011c) calculated considerably larger unfunded state pension liabilities of $2.5 trillion and unfunded city and county liabilities of $574 billion. These calculations measure the value of pension promises as streams of cash flows that must be paid regardless of market performance. While these mark-to-market gaps had widened during the financial crisis, they existed even before the 2008 downturn in equity markets (Novy-Marx and Rauh 2008).

Since 2009, there have been dramatic recoveries in the valuations of the stock market and other risk asset classes such as private equity and real estate. Indeed, the S&P 500 rose in value by 75 percent over this period, and most pension funds achieved annualized returns of well over their assumed rates of return, which were in the range of 7.5 to 8.5 percent per year. Some cities and states undertook reforms to their pension benefit structures and received considerable media attention for doing so, notably the state of Rhode Island and the cities of San Diego, San Jose, and Atlanta. Given these structural and market changes, one would assume the typical local government's unfunded liability would have seen substantial reductions.

This chapter's first goal is to provide an updated analysis of city-level pension liabilities for ten cities: New York City, Los Angeles, Chicago, Houston, Philadelphia, Jacksonville, San Francisco, Baltimore, Boston, and Atlanta. I compare the financial situation of these systems in 2009, directly after the financial crisis, with their situation in 2013, after several years of rapid recovery both in financial markets and in local government revenues.

Using the pension system's own liability measurements, which are prepared under Governmental Accounting Standards Board (GASB) techniques, I find a growth in the absolute level of unfunded pension obligations for four out of the ten cities (New York City, Chicago, Jacksonville, and Philadelphia). For the remaining cities, improvements were modest, with the total unfunded liability using GASB standards falling by an average of 16 percent.[1] This is remarkable as the assets of all the systems are heavily invested in risk assets that enjoyed a dramatic resurgence in value over the 2009–13 period. The salutary effects of these strong investment returns were offset as liabilities continued to rise and benefit payments continued to outstrip contributions. This rise in liabilities is equally remarkable given that public pension liabilities have been a central theme of public discourse in many cities for the past several years.

Furthermore, using an approximate market value of liability (MVL) approach, based on Novy-Marx and Rauh (2011b, 2011c),

I estimate that unfunded accumulated pension obligations have grown in all ten of the cities. The MVL approach uses the yield on default-free assets to value pension obligations arising from past service as a non-defaultable government bond. The deterioration since 2009 has occurred as interest rates in the Treasury bond market have continued to decline. The MVL approach recognizes that the cost of providing guaranteed fixed benefits rises as interest rates on safe securities fall. In other words, if we treat the pension benefits as non-defaultable—hence not crediting cities for their option to default on pension obligations—the burden of paying public employee pensions has grown larger for every government in the study.

To the extent that cities can default on liabilities, the MVL using a default-free rate would overstate the expected cost to taxpayers. But the goal of the MVL calculation using the default-free rate is to measure the value of the promise, assuming that it is actually paid, not to credit cities for the possibility that they could alter contractual benefit terms. Furthermore, in contrast to the discounting using the expected return on assets, it does not give the city credit for the market risk premium—the fact that the pension systems invest in riskier assets that have higher expected returns but also a much higher risk of both short-term and long-term outcomes.

Unfunded liabilities using GASB standards fell by an average of only 1.7 percent, equally weighted across cities. Total unfunded liabilities for the ten cities under GASB standards rose from $125 billion to $131 billion. Under the MVL approach, unfunded obligations have increased by an average of 37 percent over this time period. Total unfunded liabilities under MVL standards rose from $277 billion to $359 billion, or by 40 percent.

If the liabilities of the rest of the state and local government universe rose by a similar percentage point count, total unfunded liabilities on an MVL basis would have grown from $3.1 trillion (Novy-Marx and Rauh 2011b, 2011c) to well over $4 trillion during this time period.

In light of the fact that unfunded liabilities have grown even during an extremely robust period for equity markets, which was also a time when local governments were under pressure to reform their systems, the final section of this chapter outlines some of the policy options available to cities. I divide the possibilities into three categories: changes to benefit structures that would comprise a long-term solution to unfunded public pension liabilities; parameter changes that would preserve the basic structure of local pensions and have long-term effects on state and local budgets but would not by themselves be sufficient to put local governments on a sustainable budgetary path; and changes that require employees to pay more into the pension system, which I argue will almost invariably be insufficient to address the growing unfunded liabilities.

If unfunded pension obligations continue to grow, the affected cities and states might ultimately attempt to call on the federal government for assistance. In light of this possibility, I discuss several possible options available to the federal government to address the problem of unfunded state and local government liabilities. One goal of such actions would be to protect the interests of taxpayers in localities that do not suffer from large unfunded pension obligations. Another goal would be to provide incentives for local governments to reform pension systems. Such incentives may currently be lacking. Citizens may be unable to monitor and act collectively against poor government fiscal management, and city politicians may not internalize the fact that relying on the performance of risky assets to make good on pension promises carries large downsides for taxpayers. Federal measures consistent with these goals would increase transparency or provide incentives for good fiscal behavior.

Some observers have suggested the establishment of a new federal insurance agency, akin to the Pension Benefit Guaranty Corporation (PBGC) that backstops corporate defined-benefit (DB) pensions. I argue that if the PBGC experience is a guide, such a system might initially reduce unfunded liabilities but is likely to shift more long-term risks onto federal taxpayers.

I conclude with the prediction that most systems will continue to hope for high equity returns and an increase in interest rates, while politicians will likely fight battles around the first-step reforms. If the bull market in equities resumes and continues, the financial status of the pension systems will be either stable or only slowly deteriorating, buying time for states and localities. Downturns or stagnation in equity markets will pressure systems, and cities may attempt to increase revenue to pension systems by raising taxes and cutting services. How robust state and local tax bases will be to these changes remains to be seen and is an important area for further research.

Data and Sample

Table 1.1 lists the ten systems analyzed in this chapter. To select these systems, I began with the five most populous cities in the United States in 2013: New York City, Los Angeles, Chicago, Houston, and Philadelphia. I added to them five cities that in Novy-Marx and Rauh (2011c) were identified as distressed due to the high ratio of benefit payouts to assets: Atlanta, Baltimore, Boston, Jacksonville, and San Francisco.[2] Other possible candidate cities or systems to be analyzed on the basis of distress in Novy-Marx and Rauh (2011c) that were excluded were Cincinnati (not enough data), Detroit (in bankruptcy), and the St. Paul Teachers Association Pension Fund (school district only).

Table 1.1: City Pension Systems in Sample

City	City Pension Systems Analyzed
Atlanta	City of Atlanta General Employees Pension Plan City of Atlanta Police Officers' Pension Plan City of Atlanta Firefighters' Pension Plan
Baltimore	Baltimore City Employees' Retirement System (BCERS) Baltimore City Fire and Police Employees' Retirement System (BCFPERS)
Boston	State-Boston Retirement System (SBRS) Excluding Teachers
Chicago	Chicago Teachers Pension Fund (CTPF) Policemen's Annuity and Benefit Fund (PABF) of Chicago Firemen's Annuity and Benefit Fund (FABF) of Chicago Municipal Employees Annuity and Benefit Fund (MEABF) of Chicago Laborers' & Retirement Board Employees' Annuity and Benefit Fund (LABF) Metropolitan Water Reclamation District Retirement Fund Retirement Plan for Chicago Transit Authority (CTA) Employees
Houston	Municipal Employees Pension System (HMEPS) Houston Police Officer Pension System (HPOPS) Houston Firefighters' Relief and Retirement Funds (HFRRF)
Jacksonville	Jacksonville General Employees Pension Plan Jacksonville Police and Fire Pension Fund
Los Angeles	Los Angeles City Employees Retirement System (LACERS) City of Los Angeles Water and Power Employees' Retirement System Los Angeles Fire and Police Pension (LAFPP) Fund
New York City	New York Board of Education Retirement System (BERS) New York City Employee Retirement System (NYCERS) New York City Fire Pension Fund New York City Police Pension Fund Teachers' Retirement System of the City of New York (TRSNYC)
Philadelphia	City of Philadelphia Municipal Retirement System
San Francisco	San Francisco Employees' Retirement System (SFERS)

For the cities in question, I collected data from Comprehensive Annual Financial Reports (CAFRs) for the years 2009–13 for all the major
pension systems for which the city government and closely related entities are fiscally responsible. For some cities, such as Philadelphia and
San Francisco, the pensions of municipal employees are consolidated
into one system. In most of the cities, there is more than one system
covering city employees. For example, for the city of Los Angeles, I ana-
lyze the Los Angeles City Employees Retirement System (LACERS),
the Los Angeles Fire and Police Pension (LAFPP) Fund, and the City
of Los Angeles Water and Power Employees' Retirement System. The
study comprises a total of twenty-eight city pension systems.

Two important caveats arise that make comparison of the pension
liabilities across cities challenging. The first regards schoolteachers'
pensions. In New York City and Chicago, there are separate retirement funds for the teachers in the school districts covered by these
cities, namely the Chicago Teachers Pension Fund and the Teachers'
Retirement System of the City of New York. In the other cities, schoolteachers are covered by state-level plans. For example, teachers in the
Los Angeles Unified School District are covered by the California
State Teachers Retirement System (CalSTRS), teachers in Philadelphia public schools are covered by the Pennsylvania Public School
Employee Retirement System, and teachers in Houston public schools
are covered by the Teachers Retirement System of Texas. In the case
of Boston, there is a pension system for teachers, but the Commonwealth of Massachusetts is responsible for its unfunded liabilities
(Bachman et al. 2013).

In this study, I include systems that are legally supported by the taxpayers of the cities themselves. For complete comparability, the share
of state teachers' pensions that city taxpayers ultimately have to fund
would have to be imputed to the city. That is, because taxpayers in Los
Angeles, Boston, and Houston represent a large share of the tax bases

of their respective states, the taxpayers in these cities are also responsible for their pro rata share of state-level unfunded pension liabilities.

The second caveat regards county retirement systems. The cities of Atlanta, Baltimore, Chicago, and Los Angeles are all situated in counties whose governments also sponsor DB plans. However, these counties encompass a group of taxpayers that is different from those of the affiliated cities. For example, Cook County comprises Chicago but also a number of suburban areas with substantial tax bases. I do not aggregate the county pension liabilities with the city liabilities. Other relevant counties not included in the analysis in this report are the counties of DeKalb (overlapping with part of Atlanta), Fulton (also overlapping with Atlanta), Baltimore County, and Los Angeles County.

The main pension variables used in this study are membership (active, separated/vested, and retired), actuarial accrued liabilities, the discount rate used to measure liabilities, the market value of plan assets, salaries and payroll, contributions (city, employee, and other), and the actuarially required contribution (ARC). In addition to these variables, which come from the pension system CAFRs, I also collected data from two additional sources. First, I collected city and county population for 2009–13 from U.S. Census Bureau data, as well as the average number of people per household in each city as of the latest decennial census (2010). Second, I collected data on total revenue, total own revenue, and tax revenue from the CAFRs of the cities themselves, as opposed to the pension systems. I define total own revenue as all general fund revenue excluding transfers from higher levels of government. Tax revenues consist of own revenue arising from taxes only, excluding fees for public services.

In order to get a harmonized view of the systems, some data items for 2013 for some plans were imputed based on their previous year's values and the average growth rates of these data items for the other plans in the sample.

Table 1.2 provides summary statistics on these items, specifically the mean, minimum, maximum, and total of the pension variables at the plan level. The plans analyzed cover 1,188,552 members,[3] of which 619,604 (or 52 percent) are active and 543,815 (or 46 percent) are retired. The remaining members are no longer employed by the city but have left with a vested benefit that they have not yet begun to claim. The total actuarial liabilities of these plans were almost $357 billion as of 2013, backed by assets with a total market value of $226 billion, for a total unfunded liability using GASB standards of almost $131 billion. The mean discount rate used for actuarial discounting purposes was 7.7 percent with a range of 7.0 to 8.5 percent. The mean percentage of the employer ARC that plans contributed was 84.7 percent, with a range of 18.1 (Chicago Municipal) to 124.3 percent (Chicago Metropolitan Water District).

As of 2013, these plans were collectively 63.4 percent funded, with plans paying out 9.2 percent of assets as benefits per year and paying in 7.1 percent in contributions. However, there is some skewness to these statistics. The equally weighted mean funding ratio across the twenty-eight plans is 61.8 percent, and the equally weighted mean ratio of benefits paid to assets is 10.2 percent, with 7.3 percent paid in as contributions.

Evolution of Assets and Liabilities (2009–13)

Figure 1.1 shows the evolution of total liabilities under GASB standards, total market assets, and the difference (or funding status) for the twenty-eight plans in the sample. As the figure shows, these plans had $157 billion of assets in 2009 and $226 billion of assets in 2013, for a five-year growth rate of 44 percent. Total liabilities grew from $281 billion to $357 billion, for a five-year growth rate of 27 percent. Because the liabilities were starting from a much higher

Table 1.2: Summary Statistics
This table shows summary statistics for the twenty-eight plans analyzed in this chapter. The twenty-eight plans are listed in Table 1.1.

Variable	Count	Mean	Min	Max	Total
Members	28	42,448	1,841	328,579	1,188,552
Active Members	28	22,129	849	179,615	619,604
Retired Members	28	19,422	992	141,589	543,815
Actuarial Liability ($M)	28	$12,734	$754	$69,799	$356,544
Market Value (MV) of Assets ($M)	28	$8,072	$561	$47,195	$226,021
Unfunded Actuarial Liability	28	$4,662	$192	$24,004	$130,523
Payroll ($M)	28	$1,556	$40	$12,265	$43,557
Benefits Paid ($M)	28	$746	$39	$4,667	$20,878
Contributions ($M)	28	$572	$23	$3,485	$16,012
Employer Contributions ($M)	28	$477	$14	$3,047	$13,353
Discount Rate	28	7.7%	7.0%	8.5%	
ARC	27	$564	$17	$3,047	
Average Salary	23	$73,572	$37,310	$109,830	
Percent of ARC Contributed	21	84.7%	18.1%	124.3%	
% Active	28	48.7%	34.6%	71.3%	52.1%
Funding Ratio (MV Assets/AAL)	28	61.8%	27.0%	88.3%	63.4%
Benefits/MV Assets	28	10.2%	5.1%	22.1%	9.2%
Contributions/MV Assets	28	7.3%	2.1%	23.6%	7.1%
Employee/Total Contributions	28	26.3%	0.0%	71.7%	16.6%

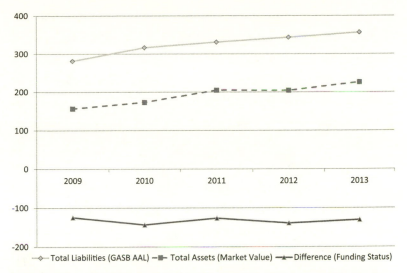

Figure 1.1. Total Assets and Liabilities of Twenty-Eight Systems from Ten Cities. This figure shows total assets and liabilities for the twenty-eight pension systems of the ten cities analyzed in this chapter: New York City, Los Angeles, Chicago, Houston, Philadelphia, Jacksonville, San Francisco, Baltimore, Boston, and Atlanta.

baseline level, the fact that assets grew more quickly did not erode the unfunded liability at all. In fact, the unfunded liability (or gap between assets and liabilities) grew from $125 billion in 2009 to $131 billion in 2013, an increase of 5 percent over the five-year period.

This is an important principle of asset-liability management. If liabilities are larger than assets, then even if assets grow at a faster rate than liabilities, the gap between assets and liabilities might nonetheless increase.

One factor that contributed to the increase in liabilities was that some systems marginally lowered their discount rates. The sample liability-weighted average discount rate fell from 8.0 percent in 2009 to 7.4 percent in 2013. For example, the city of New York employed a discount rate of 8 percent through 2009 and lowered it to 7 percent for the years 2010 and afterward, the lowest rate used by systems in this study.[4] Not all funds reduced the discount rate, however. The three pension funds from the city of Houston all still used an 8.5 percent discount rate in the 2013 actuarial reports. Without changes to discount rates, total liabilities would have been around $25 billion lower,[5] but these totals would still have grown by 17 percent. Lower discount rates therefore accounted for approximately one-third of the increase in liabilities.

Figure 1.2 shows total per-capita unfunded liabilities for the ten cities in the sample, with the liabilities measured at GASB discount rates. The top graph shows the results for the five largest cities. At the top of the graph is Chicago, with unfunded liabilities, according to the accounting methodologies used in the systems' own reports, of $21,671 per household in 2009, rising to $28,472 per household in 2013. New York City had a level of unfunded liabilities per capita that was very similar to Chicago's in 2009, at $21,264, rising slightly to $21,430 in 2013. Under governmental accounting, Philadelphia's unfunded liabilities remained steady at around $9,000 per household through this period. Houston ended fiscal 2013 with unfunded liabilities of $4,350 per household, having improved by around $1,000 from fiscal 2009. Los Angeles showed the most improvement on the measures that use GASB discount rates, with unfunded liabilities declining from $9,200 per household to $7,000.

The bottom graph shows unfunded liabilities per household, calculated under GASB standards for the five smaller cities in the sample. San Francisco showed the greatest improvement on these measures, with stated unfunded liabilities falling from around $13,000 per household to around $9,000 per household. Atlanta and Baltimore showed modest improvement as well, while Jacksonville and Boston deteriorated.

Figure 1.3 shows how flows (benefit payments and contributions) have evolved for the ten cities in the sample. Total benefit payments

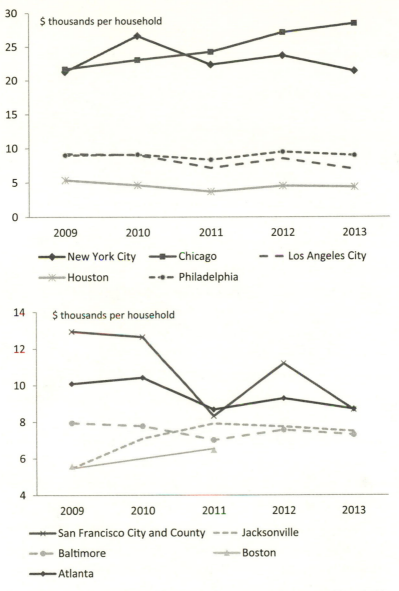

Figure 1.2. Actuarial Unfunded Liability in Thousands of Dollars per Household.

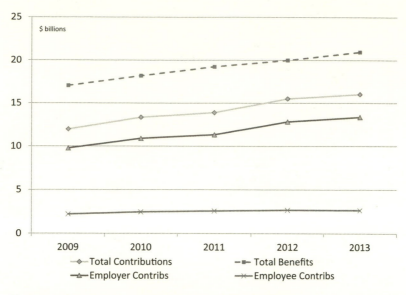

Figure 1.3. Contributions and Benefit Payouts for Ten Cities.

have increased from $17.0 billion to $20.9 billion. Total contributions have increased from $12 billion to $16 billion. So both total benefit outflows and total contribution inflows to the funds have increased by around $4 billion per year. Of the $4.0 billion contribution increases, $3.5 billion have come from the city governments themselves, while the employee contributions increased by $0.5 billion. In total, increases in contributions have been consumed by increases in benefits.

Another way to examine whether these increased contributions reflect improved funding discipline is to examine how city contributions compare to those recommended in the actuarial valuations. Figure 1.4 shows city pension contributions as a share of actuarially required payments for a somewhat larger sample of seventeen cities during the period 2000–2012. During the time period 2000–2008, there is a downward trend in the percent of the ARC

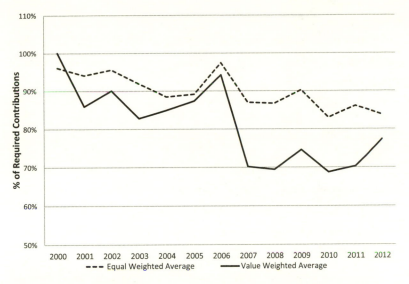

Figure 1.4. *Ratio of Actual Employer Contributions to the Actuarially Required Contribution for Seventeen Cities. The cities included in this sample and their percent ARCs for the latest available year are Memphis (23%), Chicago (42%), San Antonio (50%), Houston (68%), Philadelphia (77%), San Jose (78%), Dallas (85%), Jacksonville (87%), Indianapolis (93%), Detroit (100%), Los Angeles (100%), New York City (100%), San Diego (100%), San Francisco (100%), Austin (103%), Phoenix (105%), and Fort Worth (115%).*

that the cities paid. From 2008 to 2012, the trend is mostly flat. On average over the seventeen cities, around 83 percent of the ARC was paid in 2012. Weighting by liabilities, the average was 78 percent of the ARC. So while contributions have increased, the percent of actuarially required contributions has not increased.

Three caveats apply to the analysis so far. First, the present value of unfunded liabilities is a measure of the debt a city effectively has on its balance sheet, but does not reflect how quickly the city will face strong liquidity demands from the pension fund. Second, different cities have different revenue bases, and so they may be differentially equipped to make payments and deal with unfunded liabilities. Third, the discount rates used in the liability measures incorporated above rely on GASB discount rates. To obtain an economically valid measure of liabilities, the liabilities must be discounted at rates that reflect the fact that they are guaranteed to be paid regardless of asset returns.

Market Value of Liabilities (2009–13)

The market value of liabilities reflects the true financial cost or value of the pension benefit as of the date of measurement. That is, it is a valuation that represents the cost of buying (deferred) annuities for employees to cover all pension benefits earned by the workforce up until today.

There are two steps to converting a typical city actuarial accrued liability (AAL) into an MVL that reflects the true financial value of the promise. First, the actuarial liability concept usually includes some benefits that employees have not yet earned through their years of service to date. Since the idea of the MVL is that it would pay only pensions earned to date, the AAL must be reduced by the amount of future-earned benefits reflected in the measure. Second, cities measure the AAL using a discount rate that is set at their "expected return" on plan assets, as opposed to a discount rate that reflect the safety of a secure benefit.

To adjust the actuarial standard, I begin by determining that the actuarial measure of accrued liabilities is in all but four cases provided under the Entry Age Normal (EAN) standard. In the remaining four instances (Chicago Teachers Pension Fund, Retirement Plan for Chicago Transit Authority Employees, Baltimore City Fire and Police Employee's Retirement System, and Houston Police Officer Pension System), it is provided under the Projected Unit Credit (PUC) standard. As detailed in Novy-Marx and Rauh (2011b), the liability measurement standards differ in the extent of future pension accruals that they reflect in the accrued actuarial liability measure. The narrowest possible definition of liabilities is the Accumulated Benefit Obligation (ABO), which reflects only benefits earned based on employees' service and salary up to the date of measurement. Financial economists generally favor an ABO measure, which they then compare to the assets on hand to determine a "termination" funding status. That is, they compare the assets set aside today to the present value of benefits that have been earned up until today.

To conduct a precise conversion from the stated measure (EAN or PUC) to ABO, one needs a full model of the cash flows arising from the benefit promise, as provided in Novy-Marx and Rauh (2011c). In Novy-Marx and Rauh (2011c), cash flows for each city fund are reverse engineered based on data available through 2009 regarding the fund's stated liabilities, discount rate, and actuarial assumptions.

In this chapter, I rely on the plan-specific ratio of the stated measure to the ABO that was calculated for the sample plans in Novy-Marx and Rauh (2011c). That is, for plans that use the EAN measure and PUC measure, I respectively take the ratio of the ABO to the EAN or PUC in the data that underlie the Novy-Marx and Rauh (2011c) analysis. On average, the termination liability (ABO) is 12 percent lower than the stated liability, with a range of 5 to 18 percent.

In undertaking a market valuation, ABO liabilities must be valued using the principles of financial economics. Unless one wants to credit the local government for their option to default on pension benefits, such a valuation requires the use of a default-free rate. A precise re-discounting would use the entire stream of cash flows, as in Novy-Marx and Rauh (2011c), and use horizon-specific default-free discount rates for each cash flow. The calculations performed here are approximations based on the duration of the liability, which is estimated to be around fourteen years (Novy-Marx and Rauh 2011b).

Table 1.3: Treasury Rates (%)
Source of the actual yields is the Federal Reserve daily yield curve website.

	Actual 10-Year Treasury Yield	**Actual 20-Year Treasury Yield**	**Interpolated 14-Year Yield**
6/30/2009	3.53	4.30	3.84
6/30/2010	2.97	3.74	3.28
6/30/2011	3.18	4.09	3.54
6/30/2012	1.67	2.38	1.95
6/30/2013	2.52	3.22	2.80

Specifically, the calculation implemented to derive the liability at Treasury rates is

$$L_{Treasury} = L_{Expected\ Return} \left(\frac{1 + E[R]}{1 + r_{Treas,T}} \right)^T$$

where $L_{Treasury}$ is the liability recomputed using the Treasury rate, $L_{Expected\ Return}$ is the liability stated in the system's reports using the expected return, $E[R]$ is the expected return on assets used by the system, T is the duration of the pension liabilities, and $r_{Treas,T}$ is the point on the Treasury yield curve at horizon T.

Table 1.3 shows Treasury yields at the ten-year and twenty-year horizon, as of June 30 of each year. A fourteen-year yield is constructed as a weighted average of the twenty-year and ten-year yields, specifically 40 percent times the twenty-year yield plus 60 percent times the ten-year yield.

The first two columns in Table 1.4 show unfunded actuarial liabilities (UAAL) under the GASB assumptions and unfunded liabilities using the MVL approach (called UMVL). Note that for cities where the stated liabilities are somewhat closer to stated assets, such as San Francisco and Los Angeles, the difference between the UAAL and the UMVL will be larger than for cities where the

Table 1.4: Unfunded Actuarial Liabilities and Unfunded Market Value Liabilities
This table shows the unfunded actuarial liability (UAAL) and the unfunded
market value liability (UMVL) for ten cities as calculated using the method
described in the "Deferred Annuities Section." The systems are listed in
descending order of the 2013 UMVL share of own revenue.

	UAAL ($bn)	UMVL ($bn)	UMVL 2013 Share of Own Rev (%)	UMVL 2013 Share of Tax Rev (%)
Chicago	30.7	72.2	1015	1353
Jacksonville	2.5	6.0	730	976
Houston	3.6	13.7	710	788
Los Angeles	9.1	38.1	670	1110
Atlanta	1.8	5.2	590	660
San Francisco	3.2	15.6	584	683
Philadelphia	5.7	14.1	496	549
Baltimore	1.9	6.0	391	456
New York City	70.1	182.0	296	398
Boston	1.8	6.1	292	331

stated liabilities are already quite far from stated assets (for example, Chicago).

The right two columns show the UMVL as a share of 2013 total city own general fund revenue and 2013 total city general fund tax revenue. Chicago tops the list with the UMVL amounting to over ten years of city revenue. Jacksonville, Houston, and Los Angeles[6] are all around six times revenue, followed by Atlanta, San Francisco, Philadelphia, and Baltimore in the four-to-six-times range. New York City has the largest absolute UMVL in the sample of $182 billion, but this is less than three times the revenue base. Boston also has unfunded liabilities less than three times revenues, in large part because the financial responsibility for the unfunded Boston teachers pensions has been transferred to the Commonwealth of Massachusetts.

It is also useful to examine the flow of resources into and out of pension systems. The first two columns of Table 1.5 show contributions, in dollar terms and as a percent of own revenue. Jacksonville,

Table 1.5: Contributions and Benefits
This table shows contributions and revenues for the ten systems in the sample, listed in descending order of contributions as a share of own revenue.

| | Contributions | | Benefits | | |
	$ Billions	% of Own Revenue	$ Billions	% of Pension Assets	% of Own Revenue
Jacksonville	0.161	19.6	0.309	10.5	37.7
Philadelphia	0.552	19.5	0.746	16.8	26.3
Los Angeles	1.090	19.2	1.976	5.9	34.8
San Francisco	0.443	16.6	1.033	6.1	38.7
New York City	9.543	15.5	11.953	9.6	19.5
Atlanta	0.126	14.4	0.252	10.0	28.8
Houston	0.267	13.8	0.590	6.3	30.5
Baltimore	0.196	12.8	0.337	9.4	22.1
Chicago	0.774	10.9	3.449	14.3	48.5
Boston	0.201	9.6	0.301	8.3	14.3

Philadelphia, and Los Angeles pay in 19 to 20 percent of the general fund budget excluding intergovernmental transfers.[7] San Francisco, New York City, and Atlanta are contributing around 15 percent of that budget. Notably, Chicago is only contributing 11 percent, which in part explains why its unfunded liabilities have grown so rapidly.

Table 1.5 also shows benefit payments by city, in dollar terms and scaled by total pension assets or percent of own revenue. The scaling by total pension assets illustrates which funds are paying out the largest percentage of fund assets per year, specifically Philadelphia at around 17 percent and Chicago at around 14 percent. The final column can be thought of as indicating what percent of general fund revenues would have to go toward paying pensions if the funds ran out of money—almost half, in Chicago's case.

Figure 1.5 shows unfunded liabilities per household at Treasury rates. These graphs can be considered in parallel with those in Figure 1.2. The top graph shows the five largest cities in the sample. Both Chicago

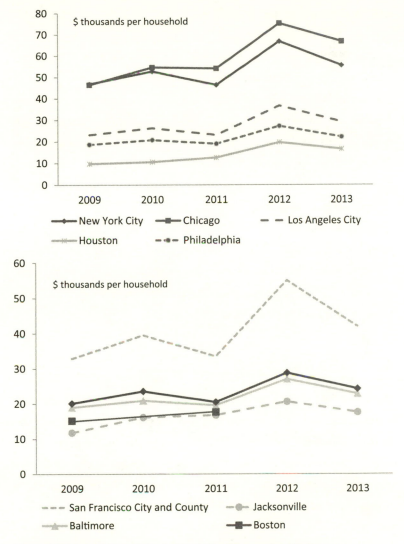

Figure 1.5. Market Value Unfunded Liability, Thousands of Dollars per Household.

and New York City began the sample period with around $46,000 of unfunded liabilities per household. In 2013, Chicago had risen to almost $66,900 per household and New York City to $55,600 per household. Other cities show similar patterns of increase.

The factor that makes these graphs different from Figure 1.2 is the discount rate, which is applied year by year. So the fact that rates were much lower in 2012 and 2013 than in 2009 affects these calculations. This highlights one of the features of the MVL calculation, namely that it reflects the fact that pension obligations are more expensive to meet as interest rates fall.

In sum, while total unfunded liabilities on an actuarially measured basis have remained about flat over the sample period of 2009–13, total unfunded liabilities measured using the principles of financial economics have increased, as the decline in interest rates has made pension promises more expensive to deliver.

Roadmap Forward

In this section, I provide a roadmap of the possible actions that could conceivably be taken by city governments. Figure 1.6 provides an overview of this roadmap. There are three main categories I consider: structural changes, benefit parameter changes, and contribution increases. There are four possible groups of claimants that these changes could affect: retirees, current employees, new employees, and taxpayers.

Structural Changes

Structural changes are those that fundamentally alter the nature of the benefit contract for some group of workers for either past or future work. These include the introduction of different forms of providing retirement benefits.

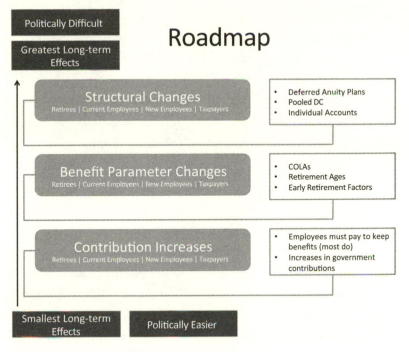

Figure 1.6. Roadmap for Municipal Pension Reform.

Individual Account Plans

The structural change that would be most familiar to private sector workers would be to move some or all workers onto an individual-account retirement plan, where workers are responsible for managing their own assets. It is worth pointing out that such individual account plans would not necessarily have to have all the same features as the typical 401(k) plans, which have resulted in some employees making suboptimal savings and investment decisions (Brown et al. 2007, Choi et al. 2011, Tang et al. 2010) and some paying substantial fees for the mutual funds in these funds. Individual account plans can be established to encourage saving if contributions are mandatory (or at least the default) and employer matches are substantial. To avoid excessive fees, plans could offer only low-cost mutual funds. To avoid under-annuitization, plans could offer the option to participants to convert their retirement wealth into an annuity upon retirement.

Recent attempts to introduce 401(k) plans for public workers have faced challenges when put to the political test. Perhaps the most well-known failed attempt was former Los Angeles mayor Richard Riordan's fall 2012 pension reform effort that would have moved all new employees onto 401(k) plans. Representatives of public safety workers found this provision particularly unpalatable and mounted severe opposition. As pointed out in a press article by Maddaus (2013), the experience of Riordan in Los Angeles contrasts with the case of San Diego, where reform proponents gave ground and eliminated plans to have newly hired public safety officials on 401(k) plans. In exchange, they received support from public safety unions for their reform plans, which included introducing 401(k) plans for other types of workers. Of course, this leaves the fire and police funds with the DB structure and likely continued growth in unfunded liabilities. The success of San Diego where Los Angeles failed may have also have had more to do with differences in funding, time frame, and political support than with differences in the particular features of the reform plans.

An approach related to the introduction of 401(k)s is to introduce a mixed or hybrid plan where new employees or some group of employees receive a more modest DB accrual combined with a 401(k) plan. This is the solution that the city of Atlanta arrived at in 2011. While the rate of growth of unfunded liabilities is slowed, it is not stopped completely unless contribution increases are sufficient to pay for the true cost of the DB portion (see "Deferred Annuity Plans" below).

An even softer reform is to offer new employees the option of choosing a 401(k) or a hybrid plan. For example, Philadelphia mayor Michael Nutter reached a contract agreement in February 2014 with one of the main public employee unions (District Council 47) under which new employees could join a hybrid plan or remain in the traditional plan and pay 1 percent of pay more than current city employees, rising by another 1 percent of pay in 2016. This deal also shows how employees might be given incentives to opt into defined-contribution plans instead of paying more into defined-benefit plans, although it is not clear that the incentives in this instance are strong enough. The city has also entered into a similar agreement with one of its other public employee unions (District Council 33), but with smaller contribution increases (0.5 percent in 2015 and another 0.5 percent in 2016).

In sum, no major city government has succeeded in implementing mandated 401(k)-type plans for all new hires. Either the 401(k) has been optional, or limited to certain groups of new hires, or it accompanies a defined benefit.

Pooled DC Plans and Cash Balance Plans

A common misperception in the United States is that all plans that do not involve government guaranteed benefits must necessarily involve individual accounts and the associated drawbacks in terms of fees and costs to individual participants. In fact, pooled defined-contribution (DC) plans exist in a number of other countries, including the Netherlands and Denmark. There are several variants of these plans. A simple example is a plan whereby contributions from individuals and employees are made to the pooled fund and employees receive an annuity upon retirement that is a function of the investment returns in the plans. Novy-Marx and Rauh (2014a) discuss these plans in further detail.

Cash balance plans, which are relatively common among U.S. corporate DB plans and have been introduced in some state plans, particularly in Texas, are in essence collective DC plans with a minimum return guarantee. These plans also have the potential to generate unfunded liabilities, but if the guarantee is modest and the investment strategy relatively safe, they offer an alternative to traditional DB plans.

Deferred Annuity Plans

Another type of structural change would be to introduce deferred annuity plans, in which contributions are used to contract with insurance companies to buy deferred life annuities for the employees, as proposed in the Secure Annuities for Employee (SAFE) Retirement Act of 2013. A deferred annuity is a life annuity whose payments begin at some future date. In fact, when an employee earns rights to a defined benefit in a traditional DB plan, she is essentially being granted the promise of a deferred annuity from the employer. There is a relatively thin market for deferred annuities in the United States today, but it could be expanded through demand from public employee pension systems.

The advantage of deferred annuity plans is that they offer a structural change alternative that might be considered by public unions who reject individual accounts and DC plans on principle, as the payouts in a deferred annuity plan are guaranteed and do not vary with the valuations of risky assets. Furthermore, in a deferred annuity plan, the city assumes no unfunded liability, as the responsibility to pay the pension becomes that of the insurer.

Such plans expand the role of insurance companies in the provision of retirement benefits to public employees. As explained in the "Federal Action" section below, the U.S. tax code may need to be amended before such plans would receive the same tax treatment as traditional DB plans.

Challenges

A unifying feature of these structural changes is that they would all eliminate the accrual of any new unfunded liabilities. Private sector pension law governed by the Employee Retirement Income

Security Act (ERISA) is particularly concerned with preservation of the benefits employees have earned up to the date of any pension plan changes. Under this principal, accrued unfunded liabilities must be met and cannot be renegotiated or impaired, while the right to earn future benefits under the same formula going forward could be changed. However, because political employee groups and some state courts have viewed even the right to earn future pension benefits as protected, structural changes might be difficult to implement in a number of states, even if they affected future benefit accruals only. New employees would be the group that could potentially be introduced on completely new benefit structures.

Related to direct political and legal opposition, another challenge facing such structural reforms is that some contributions that would otherwise go toward the traditional DB plans are devoted to the new plan. This creates transition costs, and may in part explain the opposition of public safety unions even to the introduction of 401(k) plans for new hires. If the contributions devoted to the DB plan are likely to be insufficient to cover the benefit promises made, then such a change amounts to the termination of the younger workers' subsidy for the older workers' benefits.

Furthermore, an often-cited cost of closing DB plans to new employees is the claim that the plan's existing unfunded liability will have to be paid down more quickly. As detailed in Costrell (2012), GASB accounting standards require a change in the ARC calculation method if the plan is closed to new members, and that change generally results in an accelerated amortization schedule. The acceleration occurs because the ARC for the unfunded liability in a closed plan must, under GASB rules, be measured assuming a "level dollar" method as opposed to a "level percent of pay" method.

The ARC does not determine mandatory funding policy, which is set by state statutory authorities. Pension systems that determine their own funding policy could therefore close plans to new workers and choose to pay down the unfunded liability under the same schedule as they otherwise would have. However, cities may face real constraints in switching to DC plans if legislatures or state authorities mandate that all systems in the state must make the ARC. Then the GASB accounting requirements could in fact require cities to accelerate the paying down of unfunded liabilities when they close plans to new workers, as the ARC under GASB rules would increase.

Benefit Parameter Changes

A second set of options maintains the structure of defined benefits but implements changes to benefit parameters such as retirement ages or benefit factors for some group of employees. The weakest of these changes is typically to impose less generous benefit parameters on newly hired employees. Assuming that contribution rates for those employees remain unchanged (an untested assumption) this would then amount to the employees and taxpayers paying the same amount for less generous benefits for the new hires, with the remaining savings being directed toward the legacy liabilities. For example, in 2012, the Los Angeles City Council raised the retirement age from fifty-five to sixty-five and reduced benefits for newly hired Los Angeles city employees not in public safety.

Benefit parameter changes also include attempting to reduce cost-of-living adjustments (COLAs). This preserves the fundamental structure of the DB system but changes the extent to which benefits rise after employees retire. COLAs can have a very large impact on the cost of providing benefits and can account for up to half of the unfunded liability (Novy-Marx and Rauh 2011a). Ex post COLA reductions expose retirees to inflation risk and involve what under private sector law would be a reduction in earned benefits, although this approach has nonetheless been applied in several states and cities for their pension systems. In June 2014, for example, Governor Pat Quinn of Illinois signed a law that reduced COLAs for participants in the Chicago municipal and laborers fund, including three years where no COLAs will be granted.

Another approach to COLAs is to introduce risk sharing by linking benefits to asset performance to some extent (see Novy-Marx and Rauh 2014a). An ex ante COLA change, by linking benefits to asset performance, would have a similar effect on the cost of pension promises, but would more clearly spell out legal rights and avoid the costly disputes that arise if cities attempt to reduce COLAs later. Linking COLAs entirely to asset performance leaves employees bearing inflation risk, although this could be mitigated in part if city pension funds invested some of the assets in inflation-linked bonds.

Increasing Contributions

Many pension reform attempts in recent years at both the state and the local level have aimed at requiring some or all workers to pay more into the system to keep existing benefits, or at introducing less generous pension tiers for new workers while requiring them to pay in just as much as longer-tenured workers. For example, the law mentioned above that affects Chicago municipal and laborers not only reduces COLAs, but also increases employee contributions for participants in the Chicago municipal and laborers fund from 8.5 percent of their pay to 11 percent of their pay.

These types of changes are generally more politically viable than the fundamental reforms, as the interests of the younger or newer members of the system are not as well represented at the bargaining table. However, in most cases the pension underfunding is severe enough that feasible increase in contributions from new workers will not have a major impact on unfunded liabilities. Novy-Marx and Rauh

(2014b) calculate that for U.S. public funds taken as a whole, contributions would have to rise by 2.5 times to achieve fully funded pension promises over a thirty-year period, assuming investment returns of around inflation plus 2 percent per year. Furthermore, distributional consequences and possibly labor market effects of these types of reforms need to be carefully considered.

Contribution increases, while generally seen as more politically feasible than structural reform and benefit cuts, have nonetheless been met with legal challenges in some municipalities that have attempted them. Notably, a group of Atlanta city workers is currently suing the mayor's office and the city council to undo contribution increases that have so far amounted to 5 percent of their wages and that could increase further. With the passage of time, the workforce consists increasingly of people who will be paying at the increased contribution rate for a longer number of years, which has led public employees to demand that the contribution increases be revisited. The Atlanta suit is also related to the prospect of future employee contribution increases, which is linked to the cap that the reform imposed on city contributions. Such caps can be thought of as imposing contingent contribution increases on the employees.

Dealing with the Unfunded Liability

The measures in the previous section would all move systems toward a closer balance between the accrual of new liabilities and the level of contributions going into the pension system. Short of attempts to renege on promised benefits, however, they do not address the unfunded legacy liability that exists due to the service that public employees have already performed. A possible exception to that statement is COLA reductions, which under the logic behind the law of private sector pensions actually do reduce the present value of a benefit already earned. Given the emphasis in pension law on preserving earned benefits, even if cities are able to implement new forward-looking benefit structures, they will still be left with substantial unfunded legacy liabilities. Without COLAs or other changes that affect accumulated benefits, that unfunded obligation is $359 billion for the ten cities studied in this paper alone. Such an obligation is financially equivalent to debt owed to creditors.

There are five possibilities for existing legacy liabilities.

First, the city could gradually pay down the unfunded obligations. If a city wants to pay down its existing pension debt, such a plan will almost universally imply substantial increases to contributions over today's levels. Essentially no city with a DB plan has a level of contributions today that will both pay the costs of new service accruals and pay down debt (Novy-Marx and Rauh 2014b).

Second, the city could attempt to renegotiate the pension debt with its "creditors," that is, the beneficiaries. The public sector has not yet experimented with lump-sum buyouts of pension rights, but there is substantial precedent for lump-sum buyouts in the private sector. A key parameter for any buyout would of course be the discount rate. Some participants in the pension system may view themselves as over-annuitized, or face liquidity needs, or be concerned about the solvency of the pension system, or simply have a strong personal preference for receiving their retirement assets all at once. A study by Fitzpatrick (2015) found that many teachers in Illinois were not interested in buying additional pension benefits even at fair prices; the natural question is whether this implies they would be willing to sell some of their existing pension benefits. Offering buyouts could therefore allow cities to remove unfunded obligations from their books on terms that would be favorable to both the cities and the employees. Such buyouts would need to be financed, and they would also need to be structured in such a way as to avoid adverse selection—the possibility that those employees with private information about personal ill health would be the ones to take the lump sums, leaving the most long-lived retirees in the pension system.

Third, the legacy debt could be restructured or partially reduced as part of an insolvency process, that is, Chapter 9 bankruptcy. However, such a bankruptcy proceeding by a city is only specifically authorized in fifteen states (Spiotto 2012). Relevant for this study, California, New York, and Texas all specifically authorize municipal bankruptcies of city and local entities within the state. Nine states, including Florida, authorize municipal bankruptcies of city and local entities conditional on a further act of the state government. Three states, including Illinois, have some limited form of authorization. The rules in the remaining states are unclear in that they have no specific authorization (Spiotto 2012). In many states, therefore, the rules of Chapter 9 bankruptcy can be changed at will by state legislatures, making it a politically hazardous process.

A further problem with the use of municipal bankruptcies to restructure pension obligations is that it has found limited success in achieving that goal. In the bankruptcy of Stockton, California, the city obtained the legal right to restructure all obligations including pensions, but the final plan to exit bankruptcy did not include pension cuts. This is perhaps understandable when one considers that the city still had to re-contract with some of the same municipal employees and representatives on an ongoing basis. In Detroit, city workers received 4.5 percent cuts to their base pensions plus COLA suspensions. While the COLA reflects a nontrivial portion of the value of the benefit, it is still very clear that Chapter 9 is not simply a way out of a city's unfunded pension obligations. Finally, Chapter 9 is also expensive and difficult to justify for cities on the verge of fiscal insolvency.

Fourth, the city could bond off the debt by issuing bonds and putting the proceeds into the pension system. This could potentially be useful in collateralizing the promised benefits. For cities that have very underfunded systems, such collateral might be useful as a bargaining tool in persuading employee groups to acquiesce to structural pension reforms. In essence, such an action reduces the city's ability to abrogate the funded portion of the pension liability. However, governments typically support the issuance of pension obligation bonds by arguing that it is desirable to issue debt at a relatively low rate and then invest in risky assets to earn a rate of return higher than that rate. Such a transaction in effect uses risk to attempt to improve pension funding, and the risk that the higher rate of return will not be met can be large and is seldom given much emphasis. If cities want to bond off debts by issuing bonds and putting the proceeds into the pension system, it would be important for all parties to consider the implications of the investment strategy of the new proceeds on likely future outcomes.

Fifth, the debt could be passed on to another government entity, such as the state or the federal government, through a bailout. States and cities already have complex financial arrangements through which resources are transferred, and since cities are corporate entities of the state, they can be taken over, as exemplified by the Commonwealth of Pennsylvania's appointing a receiver to take over Harrisburg's finances in 2011. There is no precedent federal government bailout of a city, but it remains a possibility.

Federal Action

In this section I discuss the role of the federal government in possibly helping to address the public pension crisis. The first question is of course what interest the federal government should have in what is fundamentally a state and local problem. Federal taxpayers could find themselves liable for city and state problems if the federal government decides to bail out a city. While some consider the possibility of a federal bailout of cities remote, bailouts of any kind typically happen in times of crisis. There is no mechanism that permits the federal government to commit ex ante not to bail out a city or a state. There are three types of approaches that I examine here.

Carrot-and-Stick Approaches

Cities are offered a (figurative) carrot or hit with a (figurative) stick, or both, if they do not implement a specified reform or set of reforms. One bill that has been proposed along these lines is the Public Employee Pension Transparency Act (2013). Under this act, cities and states would have to provide accounts of pension obligations using default-free discount rates. The stick that is used in the bill to induce compliance is the argument that municipal borrowing currently enjoys federal tax advantages, whose continuation could be conditioned on compliance with the law's provisions. Such a bill would reveal the financial costs of deferred compensation and would improve transparency in a system where these costs are currently hidden by GASB accounting.

Other carrot-and-stick approaches could involve granting tax benefits to local governments in exchange for actual reforms of the pension system. One version of this is Novy-Marx and Rauh (2010), in which municipalities would be able to issue tax-exempt pension funding bonds if and only if new workers were on defined-contribution plans plus Social Security.

Changes in Tax Code to Promote Deferred Annuity Plans

As discussed in the "Deferred Annuity Plans" section above, deferred annuity plans guarantee prespecified benefits to public employees but create no liability for the sponsoring city. Employer and employee contributions are paid to insurance companies who then provide deferred annuity contracts. In order for these plans to receive the same preferential tax treatment as traditional DB plans, the U.S. tax code may need to be amended (Walsh 2013). A plan put forward by Utah senator Orrin Hatch in the Secure Annuities for Employee

Retirement Act of 2013, and endorsed by the Urban Institute in Washington, D.C., would change the federal tax code accordingly.

A PBGC for the Public Sector?

Riordan and Rutten (2013) have called on the federal government to guarantee debt that cities issue to pay into pension systems, in exchange for reforms such as the use of a lower pension discount rate. The United States has experience with the introduction of pension guarantees and the creation of a new federal pension insurance entity through the ERISA law of 1974 and the creation of the Pension Benefit Guaranty Corporation. A PBGC for the public sector might reduce the magnitude of unfunded obligations if localities were forced to remediate unfunded obligations through mandatory funding requirements. But the PBGC experience also suggests that it would generate a new set of agency problems if local governments believed that they were backstopped if their investments performed poorly. Specifically, the existence of a government backstop for pension obligations creates moral hazard in the investment policy of the pension sponsor. If systems invest in assets that carry either systematic risk or idiosyncratic risk correlated with the fortunes of the sponsor, then the sponsor will reap the benefits should the fund perform well, while offloading the deficits that would emerge if the fund performs poorly and the sponsor enters bankruptcy.

The Pension Benefit Guaranty Corporation (2014), in its projection report for the 2013 fiscal year, highlights a net deficit of $27.4 billion in the single-employer plan and a projection of the deficit of $7.6 billion as of 2023. However, these calculations do not use market valuations. Van Binsbergen, Novy-Marx, and Rauh (2014) estimate, using MVL approaches, that the PBGC's insurance of unfunded corporate liabilities has grown to a net debt with a value of $358 billion.

Conclusion

In this chapter, I show that the unfunded liabilities of a sample of ten large U.S. cities have on average not declined despite stock market increases. On an MVL basis, the liabilities have substantially increased. I have also discussed a range of possible actions that city governments and the federal government could undertake.

Looking forward, the reform process itself needs attention. City officials that wish to reform pensions must walk a tightrope between forcing reforms and attempting to gain consensus for reforms. Forcing reforms can lead to lawsuits that challenge the validity of the new policies, as has happened with the statewide Illinois pension reform of 2013. But consensus-oriented reforms may not go far enough to address the issue. It may be that city employees only notice their skin in the game when pension funds run low, in which case there will be trade-offs of funding increases in exchange for pension reform. Cities that are committed to paying actuarially required contributions are likely to see citizens more eager for pension reform as they feel the pain of making the contributions, but ironically these are the cities where employees will be least concerned.

In sum, the pressure to deal with the pension crisis has to date simply not been strong enough from interested parties. The groups most likely to exert that pressure are citizens who feel their services squeezed, taxpayers who rebel against tax increases without improvements in services, bondholders who are concerned that their debts will be impaired to pay pensions, and pension recipients who become concerned that they will not receive their full benefits. Until now, each of these groups either has not had the collective will to act or has assumed that the other groups will bear the brunt of the cuts. Until discipline comes strongly from these groups, politicians will likely fight battles around the first-step reforms rather than badly needed structural changes.

2 The Law and Politics of Municipal Pensions

Amy B. Monahan

Introduction

Many municipalities are struggling to meet their pension funding obligations, primarily because of large unfunded liabilities related to already-earned pension benefits. Pension debt is a problem not just for large cities garnering headlines—such as Detroit, Stockton, and Chicago—but for cities of all sizes throughout the country. Much municipal pension debt can be explained by a systemic lack of funding discipline when it comes to making annual contributions to such plans. During the recent financial crisis, the problem appeared to grow larger because of the downturn in equity markets—although it now seems clear that the problem is not one that can be blamed primarily on market returns (see Rauh, this volume).

Significant public pension debt threatens the livelihood of cities and states. There is widespread agreement that state and local pension plans are significantly underfunded, and that such underfunding is likely to lead to some combination of two undesirable outcomes: (1) a reduction in benefits for plan participants and (2) the crowd-out of other governmental services. Legal issues involve both the legal ability of states and cities to reduce earned pension benefits and the possibility of local pension liabilities being adjusted within bankruptcy. In addition, a third issue is whether law can be effectively used to prevent underfunding from occurring in the first place.

Given the clear, undesirable consequences of unfunded pension liabilities, why is it that so many municipalities find themselves in such a situation? The answer, I argue, is that political economic forces strongly favor systemic underfunding, and the law that applies to public pension plans has done nothing to stem such political inclinations—in some cases arguably exacerbating them. This chapter will explore the causes of and potential solutions to underfunded municipal pensions from both legal and political perspectives, concluding with a discussion of steps municipalities can take to improve how law regarding public pension plans functions.

Why Are So Many Municipal Pensions Underfunded, and What Does Law Have to Do with It?

The Political Economy of Public Pensions

This chapter posits that, to the extent that municipalities have a public pension problem, it is caused not by funding benefits currently being earned, or by the generosity of benefits per se, but rather by the fact that many municipal plans failed to adequately fund their plans in years past. This lack of funding discipline is not limited to one or two bad actors. Rather, it is a nearly universal problem of public plans, given that they depend on political budget allocations for annual contributions.

The political economy of pension contributions in fact favors systemic underfunding. The budget process for a municipality typically starts with fixed revenue dollars that are available for allocation. All allocations must then compete for these limited dollars. Politicians who seek to be reelected should spend those dollars in a manner that is highly salient to current constituents. Pension contributions, unfortunately, do not meet this criterion. When a politician allocates pension contributions, she is setting aside money today to pay benefits due in the future. There is very little political payoff for such an allocation, particularly when compared to spending in highly visible ways on current needs, such as increasing spending on public education or public safety. Often, when politicians face incentives to spend money in suboptimal ways, there are other political or market forces to push back against the inclination. This tends not to be true in the pension funding context, since employees (the obvious counterpressure to the political inclination to underfund) are often better off if pension costs are kept artificially low. If employees were to pressure politicians to fully fund annual pension costs, there would be less money left for other forms of employee compensation such as salary and health benefits. Alternatively, if employees pressure politicians to fully fund pension plans, it might create pressure to make pension benefits less generous.

Similarly, credit markets generally have been ineffective in creating pressure to adequately fund pensions on an ongoing basis. While credit rating agencies do monitor pension debt, and such pension debt does affect a government's credit rating, negative repercussions are generally felt by the government only when a plan has become significantly underfunded. In other words, credit markets do exert pressure to address pension debt, but only when the plan is close to crisis level. There is no evidence that credit markets create pressure on governments to make their full annual contribution year after year.

Once the money is contributed to the plan, political forces can continue to create pressures that tend to lead to suboptimal outcomes. Ideally, pension trustees should invest plan assets in accordance with modern portfolio theory, diversifying investments in order to maximize return and minimize risk. Trustees should select investments solely for the purpose of providing benefits to plan participants and beneficiaries. With public pension plans, however, assets are often controlled by political actors, not independent fiduciaries. The mix of politics and investment decisions can lead to a host of problems, ranging from criminal behavior (for example, accepting kickbacks for placing investments) to public use of private funds (for example, using pension plan assets to build a prison) to politically driven limitations on investment choices (for example, disallowing investments based on social concerns, such as a ban on investing in tobacco companies). Fitzpatrick and Monahan (2014) found that municipal plans are more likely than state plans to be subject to these political pressures in plan governance.

How Law Influences the Success of Municipal Pensions

Law interacts with the political framework of public pensions in complex ways. First, there is no generally recognized legal right to full annual funding of a public pension plan. As a result, those most likely to be harmed by chronic underfunding are generally powerless to force politicians to adequately fund promised benefits through legal means. While there are a handful of jurisdictions that have found a cognizable right to full annual funding of pension plans, most jurisdictions hold that no legal harm has occurred until a plan actually runs out of money to pay the participant's benefit. Essentially what courts hold is that a plaintiff who complains about a government failing to make an annual pension contribution does not have a "ripe" claim, because we will not know whether the failure to fund the pension in a given year actually harms a plaintiff until that plaintiff's benefits come due. If there ends up being enough money to pay the plaintiff's benefits, she was not harmed by the failure to fund. Principals of justiciability require us to wait until the extent of the harm, if any, is known before we pass judgment. While one can question the wisdom of this judicial approach, law clearly has not been used to effectively enforce funding discipline.[1]

What is clear is that law creates challenges for public pension plans for several reasons. On the state level, the law protecting pension benefits is in most states uncertain, significantly hampering efforts to negotiate solutions when pension underfunding occurs. Legal protections for benefits, like nearly all other legal requirements that apply to public plans, are provided by state law. As a result, there is significant variation from state to state. Nevertheless, some generalizations can be made. A minority of states protect public pension benefits as a form of property interest. In these states, the accrued pension benefits of participants are subject to modification prior to retirement, provided the change is not arbitrary and capricious. Most states, however, ground their protection of public pension benefits in contract theory, although these states differ significantly with respect to what features of a plan they consider to be protected by the contract. The finding of a contract is legally significant because both the U.S. and state constitutions prohibit a state from impairing the obligation of contracts, thereby making detrimental pension changes potentially unconstitutional. In some states, a contract is considered formed only once a participant has retired or is eligible to retire, freely allowing benefit changes prior to that date. In other states, a contract is formed only once a participant has met the plan's minimum service requirement (or "vests" in pension terminology), and only protects benefits that have been earned. In other states, courts have held that the contract is formed on an employee's first day of employment, and protects not only earned benefits, but also the rate of future accruals, effectively prohibiting any detrimental change to the pension plan's benefit formula for any current employee. Finally, it should be noted that in many states, there is no clearly defined rule of law regarding what is or is not protected.

On top of that, even in states with the strongest form of legal protection for pension benefits, the state in almost all circumstances has the ability to modify benefits where reasonable and necessary to serve an important public purpose.[2] This standard is not, however, as easy to satisfy as its plain language implies. In determining whether the action is aimed at an important public purpose, courts look to see whether there is a "significant and legitimate public purpose behind the regulation, such as the remedying of a broad and general social or economic problem" (*Energy Reserves Group, Inc. v. Kansas Power and Light Co.*, 459 U.S. 400, 411–12 [1983]). In determining reasonableness, courts consider whether the circumstances that necessitated the change "were unforeseen and unintended by the legislature" when the contract was formed (*U.S. Trust Co. of N.Y. v. New Jersey*, 431 U.S. 1, 31 [1977]). In addition, in determining reasonableness the court takes into account the degree of impairment (*U.S. Trust Co. of N.Y. v. New Jersey*, 27). Perhaps most importantly, the state's action is considered to be necessary only when (1) no other, less drastic modification could have been implemented, and (2) the state could not have achieved its goals without the modification (*U.S. Trust Co. of N.Y. v. New Jersey*, 29–30).

Municipalities, however, have it in some ways even worse than state-level plans. In many states, the legal protection provided to pension benefits is not explicitly stated in either the constitution or statute. Rather, courts have implied the existence of a contract based on the particular facts and circumstances of the legal challenge in front of them. While there might be a state court ruling that one of the state-level public pension plans creates a contract between the state and its covered employees, that ruling may be distinguishable from the facts surrounding a municipal plan in that same state, further adding to legal uncertainty at the municipal level.

The end result of this legal uncertainty is that politicians in municipalities with significant underfunding may be hesitant to address such underfunding through benefit reductions, given the certainty that participants will challenge the legality of such changes, along with the uncertain outcome of such legal challenges. For politicians, it may not make sense to spend political capital on a pension solution that might be thrown out by a court. Furthermore, even where the parties involved would prefer to negotiate changes instead of litigate, it can be very difficult to effectively negotiate when the parties have very different views about what the law does or does not protect. A government that believes it is free to cut benefits is unlikely to have a successful negotiation with employees who believe their pension rights are absolutely guaranteed.

Additionally, in states that have clear, strong protections for pension benefits, the law may paradoxically contribute to pension underfunding. For example, assume you are a participant in the Illinois State Retirement System. You know that the Illinois state constitution provides that membership in the retirement system shall be considered a contractual relationship that shall not be diminished or impaired. You therefore feel confident that the state must, under all circumstances, pay you your promised pension benefits. Even if this belief is mistaken, if a majority of employees believe their pension payouts must always legally be made in full, they are much less likely to pressure politicians to make the full annual contribution to the plan. The plan participants may simply believe that the government will have to come up with the money even if they fail to set it aside on an annual basis. Unfortunately, many plan participants are now discovering that legal protections for benefits are not as ironclad as they may believe, and that it is not always the case that the state will simply find the money to pay benefits.

Finally, states with laws that protect future pension accruals fix the future cost of government services. Prominent examples of this situation are found in California and New York. This approach is critiqued in more detail below, but for now it is sufficient to note that such legal protection comes with the downside of fixing in place a significant part of the cost of future services, giving the government fewer options for addressing existing unfunded liabilities.

The Ideal Legal Framework for Public Pensions

Thus far, this chapter has suggested that not only does law not help strengthen and stabilize public pension plans, it can actually undermine the success of such plans. Law can and needs to be more effective if states and cities are to continue offering traditional public pension plans.

Funding Standards

Every public plan that I have examined has some type of legal requirement to annually fund the plan. What research has shown, however, is that such funding requirements are either manipulated or ignored, even where such requirements are explicitly mandated in the state's constitution (Monahan 2015). Not only do politicians ignore such requirements, they do so without repercussion. There is little to no evidence that annual funding requirements can be effectively enforced through the courts.

These funding requirements typically cannot be enforced by courts because (1) they are sufficiently vague that courts have nothing concrete to enforce and (2) courts often lack the ability to direct state funds, either because of constitutional limitations on the ability to allocate funds from the state treasury, or because potentially allocated funds simply do not exist. A recent New Jersey Supreme Court case struck down a statutory funding requirement on different grounds, finding that the funding requirement was an unconstitutional form of debt under the state constitution because it placed a binding financial obligation on future legislatures (*Burgos v. State*, 2015 WL 3551326 [N.J. 2015]).

If governments are to offer traditional defined benefit pension plans, however, they should be adequately funded on an annual basis. Doing otherwise pushes current compensation costs on to future taxpayers, resulting in significant intergenerational inequity. Pushing this expense, as the current state of public pensions shows, can threaten the ability of governments to provide essential governmental services and the very survival of municipalities.

Law can do a much better job of enforcing annual funding requirements. One option is to move away from the vague "actuarially sound" requirement to embrace a specific funding formula. The term "actuarially sound" as it applies to public pension plans has been interpreted by courts to mean *any* funding methodology consistent with actuarial standards (even where the method is explicitly chosen to lower current annual contributions) or, in some cases, simply that the plan has enough money on hand to pay currently due benefits (Monahan 2015). If funding requirements are to be legally enforceable, the term "actuarially sound" needs to be defined with more precision. There can and should be a vigorous debate regarding the formula to use; for the purposes of legal reform, the key is that the funding requirements are specific and not subject to political manipulation. In addition, enforcement mechanisms must be clearly specified and provided by the law. However, creating a strong, enforceable pension funding requirement essentially preferences these contributions over other government spending. Unlike other costs, such as employee cash compensation, pension contributions from year to year may be highly variable, potentially creating years in which the required pension contribution crowds out essential governmental services. As a result, it is advisable that any enforceable pension funding requirement allow, in certain, specified circumstances, the ability of the government to make less than the full contribution, but require any missed amounts to be made up on a short, certain time frame. Incorporating such flexibility, however, is a difficult task. Any flexibility in the funding standard presents the opportunity for political manipulation. Therefore, it may be wise in establishing funding formula flexibility to do so with mathematical precision—specifying the precise triggers that must be met to deviate from the standard and then establishing a specific formula and time frame for making up the missed contributions.

Another option is to use law to put in place structural safeguards that help insulate pension funding decisions from political pressures. For example, the use of independent actuaries to determine a plan's funding policy may be more objective (see Shnitser 2015). This option is not terribly different from the first offered, but it would potentially provide more flexibility in determining the funding method from year to year—which may be invaluable to a municipality dealing with fluctuating economic conditions. The most significant risk associated with this method is that funding would remain subject to manipulation if the actuary is not fully insulated from political pressures. For municipalities, another option is to involve the state in ensuring that contributions to municipal plans are actually made. For example, some states condition the receipt of state funds on the municipality's payment of pension funding obligations.

Governance Standards

Given the political forces at play, law should have a role in ensuring that plan investments are managed in an appropriate way, that plan trustees have relevant expertise and continuing education, and that such trustees are bound by fiduciary duties. Law should also provide recourse for situations in which plan assets have not been adequately managed. Yet there appears to be relatively little direct regulation of these matters at the municipal level, and very little legal enforcement of the duties that do exist (Fitzpatrick and Monahan 2014). Amending the law to reflect governance best practices should be an easy first step toward improving the public pension legal framework.

Benefit Protections

Law should, without a doubt, protect earned pension benefits. Pension benefits are simply a form of deferred compensation. They are part of what an employee earns through her service to the employer. These benefits are no different in substance from salary; they are simply paid at a later date. Every state's law can (and should) recognize this right.

Many state courts, however, have come up with much more puzzling rules. As stated earlier, some state courts have held that a contract is formed on the first day of employment that protects not only what an employee has earned, but also the rate of pension accrual for future service. This approach is problematic from the perspective of municipal finance, given that it fixes the cost for future services as employees are generally retained over time. From a legal perspective, what is more troubling about the contractual approach is that courts have simply implied that a contract exists from the "facts and circumstances." Laws, generally, are not considered contractual in nature, but rather statements of current policy. Future lawmakers are free to change those policies. Because of the serious separation-of-powers issues that could arise if a court were to find a legislature unable to change laws based on the finding that a law is contractual, the Supreme Court has required that the intent of a legislature to bind itself in the future, through the creation of a contract, must be abundantly clear (*National Railroad Passenger Corp. v. Atchison, Topeka, and Santa Fe Railway Co.*, 470 U.S. 451, 465–66 [1985]). Despite the requirement that the legislature's intent to form a contract be unmistakable, in many pension cases, courts have prevented the legislature from making prospective benefit changes without even trying to establish the basis for binding the legislature in such a manner.

Courts could do much better by simply protecting earned pension accruals and granting other levels of legal protection only where explicitly provided for by the legislature. Protecting only pension benefits that have already been earned is not problematic under the unmistakability doctrine because existing U.S. Supreme Court precedent states that a contract is clearly created when an individual performs work in exchange for promised compensation (*Mississippi ex rel. Robertson v. Miller*, 276 U.S. 174, 178–79 [1928]). Just as a court should rightfully protect an employee's right to cash compensation that was promised in return for work already performed, so, too, should a court protect an employee's pension benefits that were promised in return for work already performed. It does not stretch any legal doctrines, nor raise any separation-of-powers issues, to legally protect compensation already earned.

Perhaps the harder issue when it comes to the legal protection of pension benefits is how the law should respond when a plan is underfunded and the government simply lacks the funds to fully fund the plan. Regardless of the strength of the legal protection granted to pension benefits, a government may, in almost all circumstances, modify pension benefits where "reasonable and necessary to serve an important public purpose." One of the most difficult normative aspects of this standard is whether and to what extent a government's ongoing failure to adequately fund the plan should come into play.[3] Further exploration of this difficult issue is deferred to the next section.

Lessons Going Forward

The current interaction between law and municipal pensions leaves much to be desired. The laxity and uncertainty of legal rules binding municipal governments in fact contribute to the current crisis facing many plans. As things currently stand, significantly underfunded municipal plans often address their situation at least in part through a reduction in benefits for current employees or retirees. Such adjustments can take place either within a Chapter 9 municipal bankruptcy or simply through an amendment of the relevant plan terms to reduce benefits. Examining each scenario is helpful in determining best practices in addressing municipal pension debt.

The Impact of Municipal Bankruptcy

Chapter 9 bankruptcy is an option for a municipality only if the state has specifically authorized such filings. Currently, just over half of all states have statutes enabling municipalities to file for bankruptcy (Moringello 2014). Municipal bankruptcy varies from corporate or individual bankruptcy in many ways, but a key distinguishing factor is that a court cannot force a bankruptcy plan on a municipality; the municipality itself must propose a plan. If there are creditors who object to the plan, it can nevertheless be approved by the court if at least one class of creditors accepts it and the court determines that it is fair, equitable, and in the best interest of the creditors.

One open question in recent municipal bankruptcies was whether municipal pension liabilities were even subject to adjustment in bankruptcy. Thus far, however, courts have taken the position that pension contracts are no different from any other contracts for purposes of bankruptcy and are therefore subject to adjustment. In the Vallejo, California, bankruptcy, arguably the first to consider the pension issue, the court held that collective bargaining agreements (in which pension benefits were negotiated) could be rejected in bankruptcy (*In re City of Vallejo*, 432 B.R. 262 [Bankr. E.D. Cal. 2010]). However, until the Detroit bankruptcy, there was not a direct, written opinion regarding public pension benefits in municipal bankruptcy. In that case, the court directly addressed this issue and held that pension rights, even those specifically protected in the state constitution, could be modified in bankruptcy (*In re City of Detroit*, 504 B.R. 97, 149–54 [Bankr. E.D. Mich. 2013]). The judge in the Stockton bankruptcy case reached the same conclusion (*In re City of Stockton*, 2015 WL 515602 [Bankr. E.D. Cal. 2015]). As a result, it seems fairly clear at this point that federal bankruptcy courts are amenable to modifying pension debt in bankruptcy.

In theory, these judicial positions should have positive effects on the state of municipal pensions. If it is clear that pension debt can be modified in bankruptcy, plan participants should become much more active in monitoring pension funding and applying political pressure to ensure adequate annual funding. There is a complicating factor to this calculus, however. Despite the fact that bankruptcy courts have appeared to give their blessing to pension adjustments, pension benefits have been only modestly adjusted (if at all) in recent municipal bankruptcies, namely those of Vallejo, Stockton, and Detroit. These bankruptcies began with significant talk of modifying pension benefits but, when the bankruptcy plan was negotiated, pension debt was, at most, modestly reduced, while other creditors took very significant haircuts. The City of Vallejo did not modify pension benefits as part of its bankruptcy plan, nor did the City of Stockton. In the Stockton bankruptcy, one of the holdout creditors objected to the bankruptcy court's confirmation of the city's bankruptcy plan on the grounds that it was not fair and equitable given that it did not reduce pension debt while significantly reducing the debt owed to other unsecured creditors. Despite this challenge, the court confirmed the plan, leaving pensions intact (*In re City of Stockton*, 2015 WL 515602 [Bankr. E.D. Cal. 2015]). In Detroit, the city's plan, as approved by the bankruptcy court, made much more modest cuts to pensions than those originally proposed by the city, reducing accrued pension benefits by 4.5 percent and eliminating the cost-of-living adjustment in the hardest-hit plan (*In re City of Detroit*, 2014 WL 7409724 [Bankr. E.D. Mich. 2014]). The city had originally proposed reducing pension benefits by as much as 34 percent for certain pension participants (Plan for the Adjustment of the Debts of the City of Detroit, *In re City of Detroit*, 2014 WL 834766 [Bankr. E.D. Mich. 2014] [trial filing]).

Therefore, municipal bankruptcies are unlikely to affect the political economy of pension funding as significantly as we might expect in theory. In fact, the de facto protection of pension debt in bankruptcy may contribute to or exacerbate the continuing pattern of underfunding. After all, if workers' pension benefits are protected in bankruptcy and workers stand to gain in the present by acquiescing to underfunding, the strong pressure to underfund will continue to exist. Arguably, however, the working out of municipal bankruptcies illustrates that political pressures support honoring pension obligations, and what bankruptcy can do is force actual negotiations between governments and pensioners that typically do not occur when legal changes are contemplated outside of bankruptcy.

Learning from Litigation

Regardless of whether a municipality is willing or able to declare bankruptcy, the municipality nearly always is able to pass a law amending pension benefits in order to reduce pension liabilities. In such circumstances it is all but inevitable that the government will be sued by plan participants. In part, this is because the law protecting pension benefits is often unclear. Even in situations in which clear precedent exists, plan participants may believe that they nevertheless have the opportunity to convince a court to come to a different conclusion under the particular facts at issue, given that in most states the law is not specified in the constitution or statute, but is rather the result of prior judicial rulings. The possibility of convincing a court to break from prior rulings can be particularly strong at the municipal level, where existing legal precedent may be based on a state-level plan, with facts distinguishable from those surrounding the municipality.

While changes to pension benefits have been widespread in the years following the financial crisis, in most cases the changes have been limited to new employees. Such changes raise no legal issues (it is always permissible for a government to change the benefit formula for individuals it has not yet hired) and typically do nothing meaningful to address already existing plan underfunding. The only possible exception is where benefits for new hires are cut significantly, while contribution rates remain the same, thereby requiring new hires to help pay down existing unfunded liabilities.

In order to meaningfully address its pension liabilities, a government must instead take action that decreases the amount of already accrued liability. This requires reducing earned benefits, whether for current employees or retirees. To date, the most common method used by governments to do so has been to reduce or eliminate annual cost-of-living adjustments (COLAs) for current employees and retirees. The reduction of COLAs is attractive for a number of reasons. First, it offers the plans an immediate savings. Since COLAs are paid out currently, reducing those payouts results in an immediate reduction in liabilities for the plan. In addition, they appear to be politically acceptable targets for reductions. While COLAs are typically designed to preserve a retiree's purchasing power through the years of retirement, many public plans have adopted COLAs that are in no way tied to inflation. Instead, many are guaranteed, compounding multipliers. As a result, they tend to look more like generous increases in benefits, rather than a mechanism to ensure quality of life is not diminished. Given the rarity of defined benefit pensions in the broader population, reducing these benefit multipliers that are often unrelated to inflation (and, indeed, occur during years of low to no inflation) seems to be viewed as a palatable solution to public pension underfunding.

While COLA reductions may make sense financially and politically, legally such changes are often deeply problematic. Imagine a scenario in which a public pension plan provides a benefit formula of 2 percent multiplied by a participant's years of service, multiplied by the participant's final average salary. In each year following retirement, the plan provides that the participant's benefit will be increased by 3 percent on a compounded basis. Legally, there would be no basis for distinguishing between the "base" pension benefit and the specified annual increase. Both were clearly promised to the employee in return for her services, and thus both deserve the same level of legal protection (whatever that might be under relevant state law) once the service is performed. A different conclusion may be reached, however, where the statute does not include a specific COLA formula, but rather grants the pension board the ability to grant ad hoc COLAs, or where the statute specifically states that COLAs can be amended. In such cases, there is a clear basis for distinguishing between the legal protection given to the base pension formula and that given to COLAs.

Given the high level of legal protection that should be granted to COLAs in most circumstances, why is it that so many governments have taken action to reduce them, and why have so many courts to consider the issue recently approved such changes? Part of the explanation for the frequency of COLA reductions of course involves the political and financial factors explained above. The more interesting question, therefore, is why courts have in many cases allowed such changes. Some of the rulings allowing COLA changes can be explained by specific statutory language allowing such changes. In other cases, however, courts appear to take the position that COLA changes may be the "least drastic" way of addressing pension underfunding and therefore an acceptable use of the state's power to impair contracts where reasonable and necessary to serve an important public purpose.

It is important to note, however, that COLA changes are not uniformly upheld.[4] Recent litigation in Oregon illustrates some of the issues that result in courts striking down such changes. In *Moro v. State* (351 P.3d 1 [Or. 2015]), participants in the Oregon Public Employee Retirement System brought suit to challenge detrimental COLA changes that reduced already earned COLAs, as well as the rate at which COLAs would be awarded for future service. The court first made a distinction between retroactive and prospective changes to COLAs, finding that the pension contract between the state and its employees did not include future accruals. As a result, the prospective changes were upheld by the court. With respect to already-earned COLAs, the court found (based both on the facts and circumstances, as well as existing Oregon precedent) that earned COLAs were part of the protected pension contract. The state could therefore make retroactive changes to the COLA formula only if doing so passed the police power test of being reasonable and necessary to serve an important public purpose. The court found that the state had failed to satisfy this burden, both because it appeared to have failed to consider other alternatives available to address plan underfunding and because it failed to establish that the current level of plan funding "was so inadequate as to justify allowing the state to avoid its financial obligations" (ibid. at 39).

Another relatively common approach to addressing pension liabilities has been to increase employee contributions to the plan. From a legal perspective, this approach is advantageous compared to COLA reductions. Increased contributions are a prospective change and are therefore subject to less legal scrutiny than COLA changes, which typically reduce benefits that have already been earned. Contribution increases likely have not been as popular as COLA changes because they are directly detrimental to current employees' cash flow. Governments may be hesitant to take action that negatively impacts the current standard of living of their police, fire, and school employees, whereas retirees are no longer providing essential governmental services (indeed, some of them likely no longer live in the jurisdiction and therefore are not voters, either). Increasing employee contribution rates also has the disadvantage of requiring current generations to shoulder the burden caused by previous generations' failure to fund the pension plan. As a result, while increasing contribution rates is generally much safer from a legal perspective than reducing COLAs, this approach has not proven to be as popular.

A Roadmap for Doing Better

There are two critical tasks a municipality with significant unfunded pension debt needs to undertake: (1) creating a plan for dealing with the already-accrued liabilities and (2) taking steps to ensure new pension debt does not begin to accrue. For many municipalities, addressing existing pension debt will be the more difficult task. There will undoubtedly be some municipalities where the barrier is not a lack of willingness to pay down the liabilities, but rather the inability to do so. In those municipalities where pension debt simply cannot be afforded at the same time as essential governmental services, from a legal perspective (and, arguably, a normative perspective), the best approach is one that asks for sacrifices from all stakeholders. Courts have not appeared inclined to approve pension reductions that negatively impact only one group or subset of stakeholders. There is logic to this position. Employees have completed their side of the bargain, and were not responsible for the plan's underfunding. When difficult choices must be made, it is a much more defensible legal position to spread the burden of those choices across as broad a group as possible. In the pension context, this might mean small reductions in pension benefits for retirees, but at the same time, increased employer contribution rates and increased contributions from the government (potentially supported by a dedicated tax increase that would be visible to citizens), as well as either reductions in future rates of benefit accruals or increased employee contribution rates.

Once the hard work of developing and implementing a plan to address accrued unfunded liabilities is done, the next step—and one that is often ignored in conversations regarding the public pension problem—is to enact legal and structural changes to ensure the problem does not simply reappear decades in the future. There are three distinct areas that must be addressed: funding, governance, and benefit protections. In most jurisdictions, legal funding requirements are simply manipulated or ignored. There are many ways to remedy this, but they all involve defining annual funding requirements in enough detail to avoid manipulation (and, it hopefully goes without saying, defining them in a way to actually ensure adequate funding of benefits) or delegating the authority to determine annual funding amounts to an independent authority. This latter option, while attractive, may simply be impossible to implement, given the indirect political pressures even an independent actor might face. Once such a funding standard is in place, law must also provide an enforcement mechanism. Without teeth, even the clearest funding requirement is simply too easy to ignore when budget allocations become pressured.[5] Many enforcement mechanisms exist, and range from a self-executing appropriation (requiring no political allocation) to the ability to sue the government and be granted a lien against future tax revenues.

After putting in place a mechanism to ensure annual funding discipline, the next step is to ensure that the plan has adopted governance best practices for handling the money once it is contributed to the plan. There is a model law from the National Conference of Commissioners on Uniform State Law (1997) that municipalities could consider, as well as guidance from the Stanford Institutional Investors' Forum (2007). In essence, the motivating ideas behind both sources of best practices are that investments should be undertaken solely in the best interests of plan participants for the purpose of providing plan benefits, and they should be made by individuals without conflicts of interest and with investment expertise or expert guidance.

Last, but certainly not least, the municipality should clarify the extent to which plan benefits are legally protected. In some states, municipalities might not have this ability, for example where the state constitution already contains specific language that applies to municipal-level plans. However, most municipalities will not be so limited and can greatly improve the law's impact in this area. While each municipality will individually determine its own benefit protections, a popular approach might be to specify that accrued benefits be protected, but that the rate of future accrual may be modified. Municipalities are also likely going to want to address COLAs specifically. Where a municipality clarifies its law in this manner, it has at least fixed the uncertainty going forward. Courts might not respect the "clarification" for employees who were already in the plan prior to the clarification, but that is not certain. There is no harm in a municipality clarifying benefit protections going forward. If a municipality can pull off each of these three elements—funding discipline, governance best practices, and clear benefit protection—it should stand a much better chance of avoiding a pension crisis in the future. This reformation should aid municipalities in recruiting and retaining talented workers, as well as in attracting and retaining individual and corporate taxpayers. If a municipality is unwilling to enact such changes, it suggests that more fundamental changes are needed. Perhaps the municipality simply should not offer a defined benefit pension plan, and should instead shift to one of the many other options for retirement benefits that does not rely on the government to responsibly fund, invest, and manage plan assets (see Rauh, this volume).

Finally, it should be noted that while the obvious enactor of the legal reforms discussed above is the municipality itself, the municipality is not the only option. A state could, in most cases, enact law reform that would apply to its municipalities. While not popular with the states, the federal government could also choose to enter the business of regulating state and local pension plans. The federal government already regulates such plans lightly through federal tax code requirements, and could easily subject public plans to the full tax code requirements that currently only apply to private employer plans. Similarly, Congress could remove the public plan exemption from the federal Employee Retirement Income Security Act of 1974 (ERISA), which, like the tax code change, would subject public plans to the same regulation that private employer plans face. While neither of these options for federal regulation is likely to garner significant political support, expanding the reach of ERISA faces very long odds, given that doing so would bring public plans within the Pension Benefit Guaranty Corporation insurance scheme, at a great cost to the federal government. Additionally, this approach is unlikely to be viable due to these municipalities' significant deficits as compared to ERISA's rigid funding requirements.

Conclusion

The current state of municipal pensions is perhaps not surprising after examining the law and politics surrounding such plans. Political forces strongly favor systemic underfunding, while law does little to counter such incentives. Arguably, the development of the law surrounding municipal pensions has exacerbated the political problems. At this point, many cities will be forced to address pension underfunding. The choices involved in determining how best to do so are incredibly difficult and vital to the very survival of some cities. While this chapter has offered some thoughts on the legal risks inherent in various approaches to addressing public pension underfunding, I hope its more significant contribution is to emphasize that, in the process of addressing the existing unfunded liabilities, cities and other municipalities should take this opportunity to use law to enact structural reforms that prevent such significant pension debt from reoccurring. Where there is crisis, there is opportunity, and this is one too important to miss.

3 Erosion of the Foundations of Municipal Finance

D. Roderick Kiewiet and Mathew D. McCubbins

Introduction

Many American cities are experiencing the consequences of a convergence of three century-long trends. The first is the long secular decline in employment in the manufacturing sector. The ongoing loss of relatively high-paying manufacturing jobs is due to increases in productivity and to the globalization of markets for commodities, manufactures, capital, and labor. The second trend is demographic. As the baby boomers (in the United States, people born between 1946 and 1964) age into retirement, they will, as a group, become net dissavers, causing changes in individual and governmental income streams. Third, the exodus from the old industrial and manufacturing centers of the Midwest and Northeast to the newly formed cities of the South, Southwest, and West has left these older cities with mere fractions of their original populations. Where these three trends converge, municipal governments may face deficits, disinvestment, and, in the extreme, default and dissolution; having all of these factors at work creates fiscal pressures that are greater than the sums of their parts.

State governments and the federal government, in contemplating giving aid to troubled municipal governments, may find the problem widespread. If so, state legislatures and Congress may then be unwilling or unable to provide this aid. Pensions and other post-retirement liabilities for state and local workers are underfunded by as much as $4 trillion (Ravitch and Volcker 2012b). Many of the states and cities with the largest problems (for example, Chicago and Detroit) are declining in size while an ever-increasing fraction of their remaining residents are aging out of their productive years into retirement.

We predict that cities facing a convergence of these three factors have a much higher probability of facing extreme hardship, such as bankruptcy or dissolution. We have seen this historically in large cities, with various deleterious results. Detroit, for example, has recently declared bankruptcy. For those cities whose debt financing strategies are most effective, we may see them rebound successfully. For those that fail, the feedback effects of these factors will likely lead them into a downward spiral from which they will not recover. As Ravitch and Volcker (2012a: 7) write, they "cannot continue just 'muddling through,'" and they need to get out in front of the three structural forces that chip away at the foundations of municipal finance: job losses, migration, and aging.

Urban Trends: Job Losses, Migration, and Aging

Beginning around 1980, developing countries, accounting for more than three billion people, have used their abundant cheap labor, newly arriving to their growing cities, to give them a competitive advantage in labor-intensive manufacturing industries (World Bank 2002). Augmented by the rise of an educated middle class, their sizable population advantages have also allowed them to succeed at harnessing their labor abundance to compete in services. What this has meant for

American workers in labor-intensive manufactures or services is the stagnation or decline of wages, a loss of jobs, and the collapse of the companies upon which whole communities used to depend for everything from jobs to wages, benefits, and taxes. Those companies that have survived have done so by achieving impressive productivity gains, which in turn allows them to shed labor. The communities in which these industries were heavily represented have, of course, fallen on hard times.

Cities like Rochester, Buffalo, and Syracuse in New York are now among the poorest in the country. New York's population has declined by 350,000 in just the past three years, with the state's total congressional delegation falling from forty-five members in 1960 to twenty-eight in 2010. The negative effects of these job losses are geographically concentrated in relatively older cities, that is, cities built on manufacturing and industry, as well as mining towns and agricultural centers that have seen the demand for their goods fall as consumers in the United States have had increasing access to international supplies. Each year since 1985, the United States has lost an average of 372,000 manufacturing jobs (Moretti 2012). Increased global manufacturing can cause a dramatic shift in the employment makeup of cities. The decline of entire industries and the accompanying loss of income have greatly diminished the tax base of many American cities.

State and especially local government assets are, in general, more volatile than their federal counterparts. State and municipal governments typically rely on the three pillars of income, sales, and property taxes. The loss of industry and jobs has primary effects on one of those revenue streams and secondary effects on the others. The reduction in demand for American manufactured goods creates job loss that starts with the unskilled laborer. As more unskilled laborers become unemployed, there becomes a bottleneck for jobs as the supply of jobs no longer matches the demand for labor. This, in turn, leads to a reduction in hourly wages at the lowest socioeconomic levels. Eventually, this leads to migration, as many of the unemployed will leave the city seeking greener pastures. Those who remain will likely need to be supported by government programs, further draining city resources.

Unemployment at the lowest socioeconomic levels has compounding effects on almost all other jobs in the city as well. With fewer citizens in the city, there is less demand for other nonmanufacturing work, such as in food, health, and legal services. As such, widespread job losses in the primary sector of the economy can see cascading reductions in income through all levels of the economy. With an increase in outbound migration becoming more likely, there is a reduction in demand for housing that diminishes property values and, by extension, ad valorem property tax collections. As such, decreasing employment due to globalization impacts all three pillars of state and local government finance.

Outbound migration, as discussed previously, adversely affects the ability of governments to collect revenues. The logic here is simple math. Taxes are collected per capita. As a result, a reduction in the population leads to a simultaneous reduction in the potential tax base. For a local government, the problem is twofold. A large swath of local government income is tied to borrowed monies. A reduction in the available tax base indicates to potential lenders that a municipality may not have sufficient funds in the future to pay off their loans. As such, a local government is less likely to be able to borrow money in the first place and, further, the interest rates on borrowed funds are likely to increase as the tax base decreases.

However, just because the population, and thus available revenue, is shrinking does not imply that expenditures are shrinking at the same, or even close to the same, rate. First, existing fixed infrastructure, such as roads, pipelines, power grids, and sewerage, does not just disappear as the population declines and, in fact, still requires similar levels of maintenance expenditure drawn from a decreasing pool of funds. Second, despite a decline in the number of currently employed government workers that coincides with outbound migration, the number of retirees does not change nearly as quickly. In fact, when retirees move out of the city, they are still owed pensions from their work for the city. As such, there are numerous former government employees no longer contributing to the local economy that are still collecting money from the government itself, causing a net outflow of funds without even the minimal tax returns that might be seen if they still lived within the city's limits. As a result, we have seen cities in these fiscally precarious positions seek to levy pension taxes on employees who live outside of their governmental jurisdiction.

To a large extent the history of the United States is the history of migration. The migration of people from the older cities of the Northeast, Midwest, and Mid-Atlantic to Sun Belt cities in the West and South began decades ago. Previously large urban centers in these areas have lost large proportions of their populations. St. Louis, Detroit, Youngstown, Cleveland, Gary, Pittsburgh, Buffalo, and Niagara Falls have each lost more than half of their peak populations. Globalization has merely strengthened an already existing pattern, with loss of population due to the exit of manufacturing jobs quickening its pace and making the fiscal issues facing local governments that much harder to solve.

These effects, as mentioned previously, are geographically concentrated. Many of the cities seeing these types of job loss were manufacturing hubs that saw booms from the early twentieth century through the end of World War II. By contrast, cities with knowledge sectors work almost in the reverse of the case discussed in the previous paragraph, by first attracting more skilled labor, and then, as the population grows, attracting unskilled labor. We would expect these cities to have more stable tax bases.

Some scholars have argued that formerly flourishing cities with entrenched manufacturing sectors need to make a "big push" to model these newer and still-growing cities: "A city stuck in a poverty trap faces the same challenges. It is trapped by its past. The only way to move a city from a bad equilibrium to a good one is with a big push: a coordinated policy that breaks the impasse and simultaneously brings skilled workers, employers, and specialized business services to a new location. Only the government can initiate these big push policies" (Moretti 2012: 199).

It is apparent, though, that the loss of revenue caused by increasing unemployment may indeed lead a city so far down a fiscal hole that it is impossible to climb out. Big-push policies, by necessity, need extensive revenue collections for enactment, on top of what is already necessary for basic maintenance of infrastructure and provision of already existing services. As these cities shrink, digging up additional revenue may, in fact, be impossible.

The aging of the baby boomers is another major trend that negatively affects urban finances. The effects of an aging population on a municipality are twofold. While job losses and migration diminish a city government's available tax base, an aging population also produces demand for additional expenditures. Retirees in general also provide much less tax revenue than working-age citizens and, as such, decrease the potential revenue pool. Additionally, as discussed below, a sizable portion of local government expenditure is devoted to providing benefits and health services for retirees. Thus, the presence of retirees works against maintaining budgetary health by simultaneously decreasing taxes and increasing expenditures. As a result, we expect cities with rapidly aging populations to be more susceptible to fiscal problems than those with younger, working populations.

Governments in Western democracies generally provide large-scale welfare programs to their citizens, and benefits directed toward the aged are responsible for the bulk of these expenditures. The welfare state originated, and has flourished, in a period marked by both a favorable configuration of demographics—large working-age cohorts and small cohorts of aged dependents—and unprecedented rates of economic growth (Gómez and Hernández de Cos 2008). However, today, the demographic foundations of government programs for retirees have deteriorated and will likely continue to weaken. Some countries are further along in this transition than others, but all will eventually see the ratio of workers paying taxes to retirees collecting pensions, health care, and other post-retirement benefits continue to slide.

The number of Americans over sixty-five years of age is increasing by about 3 percent per year, which is four times faster than the growth of the U.S. population in general. This means that between 2000 and 2030 this number will more than double, from thirty-five million to seventy-two million, and the share of the population comprised of this age group will increase from 13 percent to over 20 percent. In the next twenty years the old-age dependency ratio, that is, the percentage of those over age sixty-five relative to the working-age (twenty to sixty-four) population paying for their benefits, will increase from 22 percent to 35 percent. Between 2010 and 2030 the number of Americans who are eighty-five years of age or older is projected to increase from 5.7 million to 8.7 million, and by 2050 there will likely be over 19 million people in what the Census Bureau calls the "oldest old-age" group (Vincent and Velkoff 2010).

Public Employee Retirement Benefits

That the U.S. population is aging has been a certainty for many decades. Simultaneous population shifts within the country are also taking a heavy toll, as states and cities in the Midwest and Great Lakes areas are losing population and income, and their declining tax base cannot support the promises made to retiring public employees. As a result, one of the largest weights that most American cities must bear is the allocation of public employee retirement benefits. According to the Census Bureau, for the past two decades the number of retired state and local government employees has been growing by 3.75 percent annually, an upward trend likely to continue. There are now close to nine million people receiving retirement benefits from state and local governments—about half the number of current employees—and this number will double by 2030.

Eighty percent of all state and local government employees are enrolled in defined-benefit pension plans and, although there are over two thousand local government pension plans, 90 percent of all state and local employees are enrolled in plans that are administered at the state level. In these plans, contributions are made to a retirement system trust fund, and pension benefits are a function of number of years employed, level of compensation received, and a benefit percentage. As an example, assuming a benefit percentage of 2.5 percent, an employee who has worked for thirty years and whose terminal salary was $100,000 a year would receive a pension of $75,000 per annum. Defined benefits generally also provide for cost-of-living adjustments. Retired public employees are legally, and in some states constitutionally, guaranteed to receive the level of pension benefits they have been promised.

Defined-benefit plans derive the revenue required to pay pensions from two sources: the continuing flow of contributions from employers and employees, and returns from invested assets. In 2012, contributions to state-administered pension funds totaled $202 billion, with state and local governments paying more than two-thirds of that amount. By comparison, these funds posted earnings of $92 billion (Becker-Medina and Brigham 2013). When pension funds are actuarially sound, projected future contributions and investment returns are sufficient to pay for the benefits that have been promised. In making these projections, fund managers can make reasonably precise estimates of the number of future beneficiaries, how long they will live, and how much money they have been promised. Assumptions about investment returns, on the other hand, are more problematic. In any case, the ongoing increase in the number of retired public employees and the pension payments that have been promised them comes as a surprise to no one. Properly managed pension funds should have had no difficulty anticipating and planning for increasing payouts, and the general budgets of state and local governments need not have been impacted.

Over the past several years, however, public employee pension plans have taken in too little by way of contributions and often have been too optimistic in their assumptions about investment returns. According to Passantino and Summers (2005), most state and local governments made inadequate contributions to employee pension plans even during prosperous times, and by 2008 they were already 25 percent short of being fully funded (Pew Center 2010; see also Rauh, this volume). Further, state and local governments responded to the great fiscal duress brought on by the Great Recession[1] by again reducing their contributions (Splinter 2011).

Contributions would not have been inadequate, of course, if returns on investment had been high. Caught up in the hubris that marked the period prior to the collapse of the dot-com bubble, state and local governments responded to the spectacular returns by increasing pension benefits without increasing contributions. In California, for example, the 1999 bill SB400 expanded pension benefits by an estimated 50 percent and applied the increases retroactively to all retired state employees. These increases were projected to require no additional contributions from the government or from employees despite the marked increase.

Underfunding was markedly worsened by the massive losses these plans experienced during the 2008–9 downturn as stock markets started to see real losses.[2] Eucalitto (2013) estimates that in FY 2013 the unfunded pension liabilities of state and local governments had ballooned to $4.1 trillion, although according to Rauh (this volume), even this staggering figure may be an understatement. In recent years public employee pension funds have scaled back their assumptions concerning future investment returns. The California Public Employees' Retirement System (CALPERS), for example, now assumes a 7.5 percent rate of return going forward, a figure still higher than the 5.5 percent deemed appropriate by Moody's Investment Services. Novy-Marx and Rauh (2009), moreover, argue that it is improvident for pension funds to invest as heavily as they do in the stock market and other assets that promise high rates of return but are also quite volatile. The more conservative portfolio they recommend would require pension funds to increase their funding levels by another third. Kogan and McCubbins (2010) make a similar point, arguing that over the past several years the major public employee retirement plans in California have come to rely far too heavily upon raising investment earnings, and have accepted too much risk in the pursuit of this goal.

In addition to pensions, public employees receive other post-employment benefits (OPEBs). Health care coverage is the largest and most important of these benefits. Yet, unlike pensions, all state and local governments pay for these benefits out of the general budget and not from the proceeds of an investment fund. As a consequence, the costs of such benefits increase as a function of the number of retirees and health care costs, and these costs are incurred in the present. While the underfunding of pension funds entails greater cost liabilities in the long run, in the next several years the main problem facing state and local governments will be that of paying for retiree health care.

The health of pension funds likewise varies a great deal from state to state. Some states, such as Delaware, New York, North Carolina, South Dakota, Tennessee, Washington, and Wisconsin, report funding levels in excess of 90 percent. Connecticut, Illinois, Kentucky, Louisiana, New Hampshire, Oklahoma, and West Virginia, in contrast, report funding levels of under 60 percent. Rauh's (this volume) estimates of unfunded liabilities are not even this optimistic.

Accounting for this variance has so far proved fruitless, as discussed by Kiewiet (2010), as regressing funding levels upon a battery of explanatory variables that included the ideological complexion of the state, the strength of its public sector unions, and the overall level of bonded indebtedness showed no real effects. When it comes to retiree health care benefits, it is similarly hard to imagine just what it is that differentiates those states that have funded a large share of these costs, such as Alaska, Arizona, North Dakota, Ohio, Oregon, Utah, Virginia, and Wisconsin, from those that have low levels of funding, such as Colorado, Idaho, and Kentucky, or, further, from the vast majority of states that have no dedicated funding source other than the general budget. This is an area that surely warrants more research.

State and local governments currently devote on average 5.7 percent of their own revenues to employee pension plan contributions. According to Novy-Marx and Rauh (2012), barring changes in policy, this share will increase to 14.1 percent if these plans are to become and remain fully funded. Rauh (this volume) has shown that, even during the bull market of the past five years, many cities have lost ground, with additional liabilities outpacing gains in asset values. Barring changes in policy, the budgetary impact of paying for the costs of retiree health care will be at around this level of cost and will occur sooner. Yet, changes in policy have occurred, as many governments have instituted reforms designed to reign in cost increases by directly cutting benefits. In 2010 and 2011, forty-one states adopted these policies (Snell 2012). In a growing number of cases, they have also been transitioning from defined-benefit plans to the defined-contribution plans common in the private sector, or to hybrid plans with both defined-benefit and defined-contribution components (Pew Center 2013).[3]

Due to the stringent legal guarantees afforded to pension holders, these measures generally apply only to new hires, and so it will be many years before these reforms yield significant savings to state and local governments (see Monahan's section, "How Law Influences the Success of Municipal Pensions," in this volume). Cutting health care benefits, on the other hand, presents fewer legal difficulties in this regard, and thus is a more viable strategy for limiting current expenditures. As such, many state and local governments attempted to retrench retiree health care expenses by requiring current employees and retirees to pay a larger share of the premiums; dropping coverage for spouses, children, and retirees under the age of sixty-five; transitioning those over age sixty-five to Medicare; or simply choosing to no longer offer health care benefits to employees or retirees (Mincer 2012).

Some state and local governments have sought to cover unfunded pension obligations by issuing long-term bonds; about $64 billion of pension obligation bonds are currently outstanding. This policy, however, is problematic. First, substituting long-term debt for unfunded pension liabilities is equivalent to taking out a new credit card to make payments on debts one has already incurred. Since this is considered risk arbitrage, the interest paid on such bonds is taxable. Usually, these bonds are issued by governments already in financial trouble, and they result in investors also demanding a risk premium. Consequently, the interest rates that must be paid are higher than for conventional, tax-free municipal bonds. Second, this practice runs contrary to the traditional normative justification for long-term debt financing. Bridges, highways, and other types of infrastructure generate a flow of benefits and revenue, so it makes sense for future beneficiaries to help pay for these projects by servicing the bonds issued to pay for them. Borrowing to meet underfunded pension obligation violates this principle, as pensions do not provide any additional revenue in the future. As Kiewiet (2010: 14) puts it, "benefits rendered by the service of retired employees have already been realized, but future generations are being saddled with the bill."[4] To this effect, the states of Connecticut and Illinois and several cities, for example, Oakland, Pittsburgh, and New Orleans, have suffered large losses attempting to fill the gap with bonds. The inability to service pension obligation bonds issued by Stockton, California, was a major factor in that city's financial collapse and subsequent declaration of bankruptcy (Walsh 2013).

Inevitably, the budgetary burdens brought on by population aging will crowd out other services. One budget analyst, quoted in Mincer (2012: 1), sees local governments as facing "a stark choice between providing core services for citizens and benefits for employees," and characterizes the tradeoff as "pills or potholes." Pension and retiree health care obligations can be met, but they will likely be met at the expense of almost all other government expenditure. This means less money for streets, lights, sidewalks, sewer systems, parks, education, libraries, policemen, firemen, and public health and safety. Perhaps the best description of the problem is that by DiSalvo (2013: 3): "As more and more of a government budget is devoted to employee pensions and health care, lawmakers must (a) raise taxes, or (b) engage in fiscal gimmickry, or (c) take on more debt, or (d) spend less on schools, roads, public transport, libraries, assistance to the poor, and other functions. Troublingly, many governments are choosing option (d), creating the paradox of government that spends more and more to do less and less."

Deferred Maintenance of Vital Infrastructure

Cities in fiscal distress have dramatically reduced the levels of public services to their citizens, such as education, transportation, lighting, water, power, sanitary sewerage, police and fire safety, and public health programs. Many analysts have expressed concern that, going forward, these governments will also fail to finance the capital projects needed to maintain and enhance the infrastructure required to deliver municipal services.

Deferred maintenance of infrastructure is both a result of and a catalyst for the confluence of factors listed in the opening sections. Vital infrastructure is absolutely necessary for continued revenue collections, as it not only provides citizens with commercial benefits and, by extension, additional income, but also provides the government assets that it can then borrow against to finance future investment opportunities. Lack of infrastructure, by extension, creates additional revenue volatility and, if sufficiently dilapidated, can cause taxpayers to relocate to more favorable areas. Yet, exogenous demographic and economic forces can incentivize local governments to underinvest in infrastructure, which then intensifies the problem.

Cities throughout the United States have already been deferring the maintenance, replacement, and new construction of vital infrastructure for many decades. The consequences of this deferral are becoming increasingly apparent. On July 29, 2014, a large water pipe ruptured on Sunset Boulevard near the University of California, Los Angeles. The resultant flooding caused millions of dollars of damage to cars and campus buildings and destroyed the hardwood floor in iconic Pauley Pavilion. While seemingly an isolated incident, for the past several years, work crews have been called upon to repair an average of four breaks a day in the Los Angeles Department of Water and Power's 6,730-mile network of water mains. The DWP estimates that its porous system loses up to eight billion gallons of water a year, likely because about a fifth of these pipes were installed before 1931 (Poston and Stevens 2015). The DWP proposes to increase the rate at which it replaces aging pipes provided that they can raise the revenue to do so.

Yet, Los Angeles is a relatively young city. Most of its growth occurred after World War II and, consequently, its water infrastructure is actually in better shape than that of much of the rest of the country, with DWP officials estimating its water losses to be about half the national average (Poston and Stevens 2015). Many older cities have water pipes that date back to the Civil War. All told, there are about a quarter million water main breaks a year. In 2014, the American Society of Civil Engineers assigned D grades to drinking water systems and waste water systems in the United States. Replacing only those pipes that are likely to fail will require over $1 trillion over the next twenty-five years (ASCE 2013).

Other infrastructure has fallen into similar levels of disrepair. In ASCE's *2013 Report Card for America's Infrastructure*, streets and urban roads, schools also received a D grade.[5] Consistent with the D assigned by the ASCE, the Federal Highway Administration reports that potholes and rough pavement conditions are severe enough in over a quarter of our cities' roads and streets to be rated as poor, and in over another quarter to be rated as mediocre (TRIP 2013). The condition of mass transit systems is similar (ASCE 2013: 7).

As is the case for physical infrastructure in general, deferred maintenance on roads and highways may save money in the short term but will likely have large, negative financial repercussions in the future.

Table 3.1: The Widening Gap Between Infrastructure Needs and Current Rates of Funding, 2014–20. Source: ASCE 2013

Infrastructure System	Estimated Need ($[2010]bn)	Current Rate of Funding ($[2010]bn)	Percent of Funding Needed
Surface Transportation	1,723	877	51
Water/Wastewater	126	42	33
Electricity	736	629	85
Solid and Hazardous Waste	56	10	18
Schools	391	120	31

Responding to poor road conditions by merely leveling bumps and filling potholes does not prevent a failure of the roadbed, a much more expensive problem to correct. Despite this, the financial backing that states and cities receive from the Highway Trust Fund and other federal agencies has steadily declined, and current levels of spending on transportation infrastructure are not sufficient to prevent conditions from worsening further.

Public school facilities, another major component of infrastructure that merited a D grade on the ASCE's *2013 Report Card*, have also experienced a decline in expenditures on maintenance, repair, and new construction. About half of all schools were built over fifty years ago, during the enrollment surge associated with the baby boom, and, as such, are nearing the end of their useful life. However, investment in new facilities has long lagged behind what is required to prevent continued and worsening deterioration. This investment, like many other types of investments listed above, also fell precipitously during the Great Recession. Overall, public nonresidential construction spending declined from about $307 billion in 2009 to $263 billion in 2013, or from about 2.1 percent of GNP to 1.5 percent.

The entries in Table 3.1 indicate the severity of the shortfall in investment in those areas of infrastructure that are vital to the provision of basic municipal services. Taken from the ASCE's 2013 *Report Card*, these figures reveal that current funding levels fall far short of what would be required to bring infrastructure up to decent levels of quality. Because the negative consequences of deferred maintenance accelerate over time, every year of underinvestment widens the gap between what is being spent and what will eventually be required to return to a decent level of service quality.

Municipal Default, Bankruptcy, and Dissolution

The fiscal issues discussed above—chronic underfunding of employee retirement benefits and deferred maintenance of vital infrastructure—are common among almost all cities in the United States. However, in certain cases, the effects of these expenses will be far more detrimental to the affected city's well-being. The introduction of this chapter identified three factors responsible for the financial pitfalls facing American cities: job losses, migration, and population aging. In cities where these three harmful factors strongly intersect, not only does municipal government face increasing levels of necessary public expenditure, but it becomes much harder for the city to raise the necessary revenue to meet its fiscal requirements.

In a previous article, we discussed asset volatility in state government revenue streams (Kiewiet and McCubbins 2014). The Great Recession, especially, has caused many state and local governments to collect less in taxes than they otherwise would have. As a result, these governments experience revenue shortfalls. The aging of the population and the migration of the wealthy only exacerbate these deficits. In both cases, the number of available taxpayers dwindles, compounding the already sizable recessionary effects. After all, without a sizable tax base, revenue volatility increases. This, in turn, leads to additional incentives to both underfund pensions and underinvest in infrastructure. This can then snowball into a situation in which underinvestment and underfunding cause even more migration out of the city, further decreasing the tax base and, again, incentivizing further underinvestment. Where the confluence of these factors is at its peak, we can expect cities to brush with bankruptcy, fully enter bankruptcy, or be dissolved entirely.

Beginning with Vallejo, California, in 2009, several cities have declared bankruptcy, with the most notable being Detroit in July 2013. The declaration of bankruptcy is unappealing for cities, and even the threat that a city might go bankrupt injures its credit rating and casts a pall on investment (for a discussion, see Monahan's section, "The Impact of Municipal Bankruptcy," in this volume). However, the measures cities have taken to avoid bankruptcy—radical cuts in basic services and round after round of tax rate increases—are counterproductive and can be far more deleterious in their consequences than the formal recognition of bankruptcy. Streetlights may be extinguished or removed entirely. Streets may go unpaved and parks and schools closed. Some cities have cut police forces so drastically that they can no longer offer meaningful service in terms of either crime prevention or response to reported crimes. The affluent can hire private security patrols, but the poor cannot afford this "luxury."

When cities fail to provide a modicum of basic municipal services, those that can move out, do. Those that cannot, suffer. Also, while bankruptcy is an unfavorable circumstance, allowing infrastructure to fall into disrepair may be worse, in both the short and the long term. This can propel a city into a death spiral of higher tax rates, falling revenue, and further cuts. If the city then still declares bankruptcy, any benefits that might have been gained through bankruptcy protection have been forfeited, and the city is in an even worse spot. As Ravitch and Volcker (2012a: 10) write, "These pressures call into question the ability of local governments to make communities safe and attractive, and to support economic growth. As the mayor of Rochester testified in 2012, 'Before we get to the point of financial failure, we will do substantial damage to the cultural and social environment that makes . . . cities an attractive place to live. Cultural and social bankruptcy precedes financial bankruptcy.'"

Detroit, the largest city to go bankrupt, offers an abject cautionary tale. Its path to bankruptcy began, and was clear to see, several decades ago. Punishingly high tax rates and draconian cuts in services, however, produced precisely the death spiral that Chapter 9 bankruptcy was intended to prevent. Those who were able to fled. The rate of population loss accelerated and the property tax base evaporated. For those lacking the means to leave the city, the consequences have been disastrous (LeDuff 2013).

Beyond bankruptcy is dissolution. Dissolution is neither unique nor new. Anderson (2012) lists more than five hundred municipalities, across almost every state, that have been dissolved or approved for dissolution since 1920 (and the list does not include mergers, reorganizations, and so on). Michigan and Rhode Island have recently reformed their legislation governing state receivership for local governments in crisis. Pennsylvania, with 2,561 municipalities and townships—several of which are quite small—has recently amended its laws permitting economically distressed municipalities to dissolve their borders and hand local authority to a state designee (Anderson 2012). In hard-pressed upstate New York, Buffalo tried to disincorporate itself in 2004 so that it could shift some of its expenses (mainly on Medicaid) to Erie County, although the state did not allow it to do so. Many states have widespread exposure to local debt, such as Texas, where the approximately four thousand local government entities account for 87 percent of the public debt (Ravitch and Volker 2012a).

This is not to say that cities can never pull out of a fiscal death spiral. Recovery is possible. Strategies and examples of revitalization exist, but they require collective action and will.[6] Some of the most economically devastated urban areas in the country—places like the South Bronx—have experienced or at least are beginning to experience significant economic recovery, rising incomes, and increasing property values (Clarke 2015). This is possible, in large measure, because these areas have suffered such great losses of population that they offer businesses and developers very attractive real estate prices in what are otherwise very good locations. These developments in turn lead to substantial improvements in the city's fiscal outlook. In our view, municipal bankruptcy can hasten the process of recovery, making it a better option than never-ending cuts in municipal services.

Prognosis

Over the next few decades many cities in the United States, large, medium, and small, will confront dire and deteriorating fiscal circumstances. They can potentially reduce the burden of unfunded pension liabilities by declaring bankruptcy, but bankruptcy is extremely unpalatable and may not significantly reduce their financial burdens going forward. Potentially, budgetary duress could induce government agencies to achieve efficiency gains in service delivery. There are in fact some examples of cities and other local government agencies doing more with less. Local governments can provide more and better service at lower prices by bidding out garbage removal, ambulance services, and other tasks to private firms. Privatization, however, is anathema to public sector unions, and collective bargaining agreements typically include strong guarantees that any privatization of municipal services will be extremely limited. One should thus not expect too much from local government efforts to eliminate inefficiency (also known as waste, fraud, and abuse), assuming that they are motivated to do so.

In the long run, expenditures on pensions and other retirement benefits could be reduced without reducing the benefits of current retirees by not hiring as many new employees and compensating those who are hired with lower wages and lower pension benefits. Eventually there will be fewer public employees retiring, and, because their final years of compensation will be lower, they will receive smaller pension payments. Such savings will, over time, bend the cost curve on retirement benefits downward and potentially restore public employee funds to a considerably more sound actuarial status.

Such a policy of budgetary "decrementalism" is no panacea—far from it. It means that for the next couple of decades at least, in order to pay public sector retirees the benefits they were promised, what services cities and other local governments do provide will be generated by a smaller, overstretched work force receiving lower wages and benefits than those given to the previous generation of employees. We can further anticipate, for many years down the road—particularly in those cities that have large pension funding gaps—inadequate capital spending and the continuing degradation of basic infrastructure. Such policies may, in the long run, allow cities to escape from the fiscal woods in which they currently find themselves. By making the city a less attractive place to live, however, it seems to us that they are much more likely to be counterproductive.

Conclusion:
A Call for Transparency

Robert P. Inman and Susan M. Wachter

Central to this book—and troubling for anyone trying to draw a conclusion from it—is the uncertainty of future projections on the acknowledged problem of the underfunding of municipal pension obligations. As Joshua D. Rauh, Amy B. Monahan, D. Roderick Kiewiet, and Mathew D. McCubbins have ably demonstrated, there is ample cause for concern about unfunded pension liabilities.

Decisions made today in ignorance of future costs cannot be undone. To some extent, the lack of knowledge of the costs of today's decisions is inevitable. Uncertainty is a fact of life and particularly so in the actuarial world. The magnitude of the problem of underfunding depends in part on fragile assumptions about the future path of the economy and the political process. But to the extent that this uncertainty stems from opaque policymaking and private information, it is resolvable. The first step, therefore, must be to make informed decisions possible. Transparency is a necessary foundation for the important task of putting our urban economies back on sound fiscal footing. The authors of the chapters of this volume show what happens in the absence of transparency. Here we make the positive case for transparency.

Uncertainty about municipalities' future indebtedness due to unfunded pension obligations is both a cause and a consequence of what we see as the core issue: the lack of transparency on the costs to taxpayers for benefits promised today.

The lack of public knowledge of the full extent of obligations enables kick-the-can-down-the-road postponement of necessary decisions. Rather than putting into place incremental solutions that work to resolve indebtedness over time, the result may be that no good solution is possible. While crises can lead to clear thinking about alternatives, in this case, crisis means that all parties—pension holders, taxpaying citizens, and debt holders—are worse off; the sad lesson learned from Detroit and Greece. Once the problem of unfunded liabilities brings a city to the point of financial crisis, there is no going back. The city itself will have to cut back on necessary investment for future growth. This hurts all parties but may be inevitable if the problem is not addressed when solutions that do not involve drastic cutbacks in investing for the future are still possible.

What Is the Problem?

The issue of unfunded pension liabilities is a major problem for many of the nation's cities. For example, in Chapter 1, Joshua Rauh calculates that, with a long-term rate of return of 5 percent,[1] half of Chicago's income may have to go to pay for pensions. If you make a similar calculation for Philadelphia, 25 percent of the city's own revenues will have to go to pensions if it is going to meet these obligations without external aid. In the cases of Boston and New York, this obligation is roughly 15 percent of annual revenues.

Chicago is an extreme scenario. A middle-class family or firm that has options to choose where to locate gives the city $2.00. One dollar is immediately allocated to the unfunded pension liability, and one dollar remains for public services. To be attractive to new residents, each dollar of new taxes has to return to each family at least twice its cost in benefits; that's a very high threshold for city services to have to meet. Rob Dubow, Philadelphia's director of finance, has estimated a threshold of 1.3 as a benefit-to-cost ratio, which means that Philadelphia needs a return of at least 30 cents above that cost of a dollar of benefits for that dollar to be justified to households and firms that choose to locate in the city (Dubow 2014). Similarly, Boston and New York have aimed for a benefit-to-cost ratio of 1.2. Thus, it is nearly impossible for a city such as Chicago to provide a sufficient level of essential services while simultaneously covering unfunded pension liabilities.

Rauh also shows how some cities have tried to address this kind of obligation—for example, by paying down some of the debt over time, instituting structural changes to the nature of the benefit contracts or parameter changes such as to retirement ages or benefit factors, increasing contributions, renegotiating legacy debt, declaring bankruptcy, borrowing, or hoping for a bailout. All solutions require the costs to be paid by someone, and in none of the examples he cites, in fact, is the problem resolved. The costs are simply too high for policymakers to risk imposing them on the population, absent economic or political pressure to do so.

Such pressure will only exist when the underfunding is transparent enough for voters, pension recipients, bondholders, and new residents to see it in enough time to take action before a crisis is at hand.

Who Is This a Problem For?

Dealing with past underfunding is largely a question of the distribution of the pain, either over time with policies that recognize the need to incrementally decrease unfunded liabilities or all at once in the moment of crisis. Pensions are a liability, and ultimately someone is going to have to satisfy the obligation. Current residents and tax-payers will be hit in the form of higher taxes or lower-quality services. Likewise, after it becomes well known that the unfunded liability exists, the liability is going to shift back onto property values. Given these municipalities' budgetary constraints, once the extent of the liability is known, firms and households will not move into a city unless they can be absolutely certain that they will get $2.00 in benefits for every $2.00 they pay. If this threshold is unattainable, they will offer less for the property in that city or state, which will negatively impact property owners and the city's tax base.

The share that public employees will bear cannot cover the full unfunded liability. As shown by Amy Monahan in Chapter 2, significantly lowering benefits for current retirees has not yet been implemented as a feasible option. The likelihood of facing lawsuits from pension holders is significant enough to deter politicians from making large and therefore controversial changes. The political economy of pensions is directed in favor of these present considerations as opposed to future ones. Most municipalities have laws requiring current claimholders to receive their promised benefits.

Monahan's analysis further shows how the lack of transparency allows myopic decision making to occur, but the charade can only last as long as the problem remains in the shadows. Eventually, these liabilities will be realized, and future residents and taxpayers will experience lower-quality services and higher taxes when they move into this type of city. Once pension liabilities are made transparent to a population and remain unaddressed, that city will not be an attractive destination. Rather, people will choose to move to a location where they receive services commensurate with their taxes. Moreover, as people choose to move away from less productive locations to avoid unfunded pensions, society as a whole will lose the productivity of those locations that faced the large unfunded liabilities.

In Chapter 3, D. Roderick Kiewiet and Mathew McCubbins demonstrate how this kind of migration can and has hollowed out cities, draining tax revenue and further dampening productivity in a vicious, reinforcing cycle that deprives local governments of investment, jobs, and the working-age population they so desperately need. Without tax revenue, Kiewiet and McCubbins show, localities have tried to shore up their deficits by slashing spending, which worsens public services and infrastructure and makes the cities less attractive to the productive workers on which the aging baby boomers depend.

Neither bankruptcy nor a bailout can be relied on to fully resolve this underlying tension. In the case of bankruptcy, credit rating downgrades and unpaid claims further reduce the incentive for investment and in-migration, deepening the loss of revenue. In the case of a bailout, the most impacted individual is the nonresident taxpayer, who has not and will not receive any benefit from this taxation. Furthermore, bailouts become an invitation to repeat the process. Hence, the refusal to bail out may be viewed as a means to send a signal that the moral hazard of unfunded pensions will not be tolerated.

What Does This Mean Economically?

Ultimately this is a problem for cities to solve themselves. What are the implications of ignoring the extent of underfunding of pension obligations for the future of the city?

The first outcome is a direct result of asymmetrical information. The municipality is fully aware that it is creating the unfunded liability, but it is not divulging that information, thus engendering an asymmetry of information. What are the implications of this scenario? Economically, underfunding subsidizes the hiring of an excess of public employees, as hiring costs will not match output for that city. Suppose that the normal cost of the pension plan is 10 percent for a salary of $50,000. Although the pension plan requires $5,000 in funding, if the hiring party does not fund the plan and hires a worker for $45,000, the outcome is a 10 percent subsidy in the purchase of labor. As a result, too much labor is going to be purchased, resulting in higher taxpayer obligations in the city that takes this route, compared to such obligations in other cities.

The second result is a dynamic one. Uncertainty surrounding future taxes for people thinking of locating in this city will discourage such location and discourage productive investment. The cycle of underfunding and hiring is then exacerbated as the tax base deteriorates.

Finally, giving this subsidy to public employees in terms of their retirement income (perhaps not unlike Social Security) will lead to an incentive for reduced savings behavior. Adding to Amy Monahan's discussion in Chapter 2, the legal protections granted to pension plans and the currently unfunded liabilities need to be made widely available so that public employees can fairly plan for retirement.

On all three counts, potential allocated consequences emerge that could pose a threat in the future. The incentives to engage in underfunding reflect a prisoner's dilemma among taxpayers: "Why should I fund my pension if I'm going to move to a new location where they haven't funded their pension?" Such logic leads to a trend of taxpayers ignoring their own local pension liabilities in order to protect themselves. The implication is not that there will only be underfunding in one city, but rather that underfunding will be more universal.

How to Solve This Issue?

What are potential solutions to this issue? From the economist's perspective, if the problem is asymmetric information, the answer is to provide information. In a full-information world, all three of the aforementioned problems can be avoided. This allows public labor markets to recognize the true marginal cost of their purchases and will lead to a more efficient allocation of resources. But how can this be implemented?

The most important aspect of providing information is that it comes from a credible source so that the recipients of the information believe it to be true. One family knowing that there is a $40,000-per-family unfunded pension liability in Chicago does not enable that family to buy a $500,000 house for $460,000; that family is not going to get the house by telling the seller or other bidders of the $40,000-per-family pension liability. For the information to have a meaningful effect, it must come from a more credible source than one self-interested purchaser.

However, the question remains: Who will serve as that source? It is essential that the source be independent. Richard Ravitch and Paul Volcker formed the State Budget Crisis Task Force to provide such sources for a variety of states. However, to date, there is no single source for this vital information for cities.

More broadly, this information must be provided to a marketplace for current taxpayers, future taxpayers, and public employees. Amy Monahan has noted that perhaps the "best" result of the Detroit bankruptcy was that suddenly public employees realized that they might not receive their pensions (Monahan 2014). These employees and investors, either in bond markets or in real estate, are going to be attentive to the final outcome. If this information is made public and municipalities do not react, this will detrimentally affect the municipalities' abilities to raise funds. But the trade-offs faced in crisis are far worse than they would be if the crisis had not been allowed to worsen over time.

Ultimately, the economics perspective dictates that it is critical to disseminate this information to the marketplace. For example, clearly presenting liability calculation methodologies and realistic interest rate assumptions can enable all involved parties to understand and ultimately trust estimates of unfunded pension liabilities. This could allow real estate markets and bond markets to react accordingly and provide the discipline that has been lacking in the past. The longer this information is not forthcoming, the larger the problem may grow. Kicking the can down the road has in many cities increased underfunding. While the availability of this information will not immediately balance pension underfunding, it will impel all involved parties to work toward developing feasible budgetary solutions and prevent these liabilities from further increasing and undermining the future of the city itself.

Notes

Chapter 1

1. Boston was excluded from this calculation, as the data were only available through January 1, 2012.

2. Atlanta was not analyzed in Novy-Marx and Rauh (2011c) due to insufficient data at the time.

3. For comparison, this is around half of the 2,042,253 members covered in the seventy-seven cities and counties analyzed in Novy-Marx and Rauh (2011c).

4. Nonetheless, the *New York Times* reported the following quote from Mayor Michael Bloomberg: "The actuary is supposedly going to lower the assumed reinvestment rate from an absolutely hysterical, laughable 8 percent to a totally indefensible 7 or 7.5 percent" (Walsh and Hakim 2012).

5. As explained in the "Deferred Annuity Plans" section, the exact change in liability for a change in discount rate can be approximated using the duration (or weighted average maturity) of the pension liabilities. For a fourteen-year duration, for example, the $356 billion in total liabilities in 2013 would, under the lower discount rate, be worth $(\$356.5) * (1.074)^{14}/(1.080)^{14} = \$329.8$, or $27 billion less. For a twelve-year duration, replacing the fourteen-year exponentiation with twelve, it would be $23 billion less. Due to convexity, the actual decrease in value for the higher rate is less than what is implied by the duration approximation.

6. Note that this includes the Los Angeles Water and Power Department pension liabilities, with the operating cash flow of the department included in the denominator as revenues.

7. Tatum (2013) finds 18 percent excluding the City of Los Angeles Water and Power Employees' Retirement System.

Chapter 2

1. Law also shapes the obligations that pension plan trustees owe to plan participants. Law determines the makeup of the pension board; specifies board qualifications, training, and duties; and sets the boundaries on permissible investments. Law should also provide for enforcement mechanisms when trustees fail to live up to these

obligations. While one study found that municipal pension plans often fail to have sufficient governance mechanisms or enforcement provisions in place, the extent to which such failure impacts the ultimate success of municipal pensions is less clear (Fitzpatrick and Monahan 2014).

2. While a state, as sovereign, has the power to protect the health, safety, and welfare of its citizens (referred to as its "police power"), and the state cannot contract away such power, the Illinois Supreme Court recently held that a state constitutional provision protecting pension benefits as contractual in nature effectively prevented the state from using its police power to adjust pension benefits (*In re Pension Reform Litigation*, 32 N.E.3d 1 [Ill. 2015]). Essentially, the court held that the state, as sovereign, had bound itself through the constitution in a manner that foreclosed a police power argument. There are no other cases with similar holdings, so it remains to be seen whether other states with specific constitutional protection of pension benefits would employ similar reasoning.

3. In the recent Illinois Supreme Court ruling prohibiting the state from relying on its police power to reduce pension benefits, the court appeared to give great weight to the fact that the Illinois legislature had, for years, systemically underfunded the state's pension plans (*In re Pension Reform Litigation*, 32 N.E.3d 1 [Ill. 2015]).

4. For example, an Illinois trial court recently held that COLA reductions in two of the City of Chicago's pension plans were unconstitutional on the basis that COLAs were a protected part of the pension contract under the Illinois state constitution, and because, according to the Illinois Supreme Court, the constitutional language protecting pension benefits was not subject to any reservation of sovereign powers—precluding the use of any police power arguments (*Jones et al. v. Municipal Employees Annuity & Beneficiary Fund*, 14 CH 20027 [Ill. Cir. Ct. 2015]). The City of Chicago is appealing the ruling.

5. While this chapter is focused on municipal pensions, it should be noted that attempts to put legally-binding funding requirements in place at the state level may be impermissible under a state's constitutional prohibition on the creation of debt. The New Jersey Supreme Court recently struck down a state funding requirement on such grounds. In some states, municipalities are bound by similar limitations on debt.

Chapter 3

1. The Great Recession exposed the fragility of state and local government finance. Each of the three primary revenue streams available to state and local governments was impacted by the downturn. Sales tax revenues declined first, followed shortly by a sharper decline in income tax revenue. Then, in 2010, when sales and income tax revenues had begun to recover, the third and perhaps most important pillar of state government finance, property taxes, did not—three years after the economy had bottomed out, property tax revenues were 1 percent lower than at the

trough of the recession. In real terms, state tax revenues, as well as state and local government consumption and investment, were 5 percent lower in 2012 than in 2008. In all previous post-war recessions, real revenues and expenditures were significantly higher this far into the post-recession period (Harris 2013; Harris and Shadunsky 2013; Chernick et al. 2013). The pattern of budgetary havoc wreaked by the Great Recession was uneven, with some states suffering much larger losses of revenue than others (Kiewiet and McCubbins 2014). For example, states with large extractive industries, riding the shale oil boom and the general rise in mineral prices, experienced relatively small shortfalls or even increases in revenue, while states that relied heavily on tax collected on realized capital gains did not.

In the early years of the Great Recession, the federal government provided state and local governments considerable budgetary relief but, as federal assistance ended and state revenues remained depressed, states increased tax rates and most state and local governments also cut expenditures and employment. By the end of 2012, state and local government employment was 3.5 percent lower than what it had been in mid-2008. When the education sector is excluded, the decline in the number of state employees is 6 percent (Dadayan and Boyd 2013).

The immediate budgetary problems facing states today are less daunting than they were in 2009. Expenditure cuts and increases in revenue have reduced the overall size of budgetary shortfalls from $191 billion in FY 2009 to $55 billion in FY 2013 (Oliff et al. 2012). Yet cities, counties, and school districts continue to face revenue shortfalls due to falling property tax collections and cuts in state government assistance (American Cities Project 2012). Goldsmith's (2010: 1) assessment of the predicament these governments face is straightforward and succinct: "The steady increase in the quantity and cost of public services, coupled with the needs of an aging population and public pension costs have produced a long term, structural deficit."

2. Public employee pension plans typically use three-year moving averages to calculate rates of returns, which are then used to calculate required contribution levels. This significantly reduced the losses reported during 2008–9, but because these losses were necessarily carried forward, most reported losses or very meager returns well after the major stock indices had recovered.

3. In the private sector the vast majority of retirement plans are defined-contribution plans, such as the 401(k). Employees typically have a range of investment choices, e.g., mutual stock funds, bond funds, or annuities, but in any case, the retirement benefits they receive depend upon how well their investments perform, and so by definition such plans can be neither underfunded nor overfunded.

4. Retirement benefits are deferred compensation, which means that underfunding retirement benefit obligations is just another form of government borrowing. But underfunding public employee pensions destroys the temporal alignment of costs and benefits. The benefits rendered by the service of retired employees have

already been realized. Future generations are saddled with the bill for these benefits, which they of course cannot and will not receive.

5. A D grade means that "The infrastructure is in poor to fair condition and mostly below standard, with many elements approaching the end of their service life. A large portion of the system exhibits significant deterioration. Condition and capacity are of significant concern with strong risk of failure" (ASCE 2013: 11). The overall grade for infrastructure in general was D+, with relatively good grades assigned to bridges (C+), solid waste facilities (B–), and rail (C+). Railroad service in the United States is primarily freight rail and thus largely in the private sector. In contrast to most areas of public sector infrastructure, the railroads have benefited from a large wave of new investment and have become increasingly competitive with motor freight.

6. See Wachter and Ding 2014.

Conclusion

1. The *Wall Street Journal* points to a survey of public pension experts who believe 5.9 percent is the best estimate of this return going forward (Biggs 2015).

Contributors

Robert P. Inman is the Richard King Mellon Professor of Finance at the Wharton School, as well as a professor of business economics and public policy and professor of real estate. His primary research interests include public finance, urban fiscal policy, and political economy. He is a research associate for the National Bureau of Economic Research and has been a visiting senior research economist for the Federal Reserve Bank of Philadelphia for a number of years. He has been an adviser to the City of Philadelphia, the State of Pennsylvania, the U.S. Treasury, the U.S. Department of Education, the U.S. Department of Housing and Urban Development, the Republic of South Africa, and the National Bank of Sri Lanka on matters of fiscal policy.

D. Roderick Kiewiet is a professor of political science at Caltech. Much of his work uses empirical analyses to better understand questions in formal political theory. His current research focuses on the level and distribution of public school funding across the United States over the past thirty years and on the fiscal challenges facing state and local governments. In 1992, Kiewiet received, with Mathew D. McCubbins, the Gladys M. Kammerer Award from the American Political Science Association for *The Logic of Delegation*. He has written four books and dozens of articles, and he has served on several editorial boards and executive councils.

Mathew D. McCubbins is Ruth F. De Varney Professor of Political Science and a professor of law at Duke University. An interdisciplinary scholar whose work explores the intersections of law, politics, and political economy, McCubbins has published more than 125 articles, six books, and has edited eight additional books in political science, public policy, law, computer science, cognitive science and psychology, economics, and biology. In addition to a joint appointment in Duke University's Department of Political Science and in the law school, he is also the director of the Center on Democracy and the Rule of Law in the Duke University School of Law.

Amy B. Monahan is a professor of law at the University of Minnesota Law School, where she teaches and writes in the areas of health and retirement plan regulation and policy. She earned her B.A. from the Johns Hopkins University and her J.D. from Duke University School of Law. In 2013, she was awarded the American Law Institute's Young Scholars Medal in recognition of her work's potential to influence improvements in the law.

Joshua D. Rauh is a professor of finance at the Stanford Graduate School of Business and a Senior Fellow at the Hoover Institution. He was awarded the 2006 Brattle Prize for his outstanding research paper on corporate finance, published in the *Journal of Finance*, "Investment and Financing Constraints: Evidence from the Funding of Corporate Pension Plans." In 2011 he won the Smith Breeden Prize for his outstanding research paper on capital markets, also published in the *Journal of Finance*, "Public Pension Promises: How Big Are They and What Are They Worth?" coauthored with Robert Novy-Marx. Rauh's research on state and local pension systems in the United States has received national media coverage in outlets such as the *Wall Street Journal*, the *New York Times*, the *Financial Times*, and *The Economist*. Rauh received a B.A. degree in economics from Yale University and a Ph.D. in economics from the Massachusetts Institute of Technology.

Richard Ravitch, a former New York State lieutenant governor, is a lawyer, businessman, author, and public official who has been engaged in the private and public sectors for more than fifty years. He began his career in the construction business as a principal of the HRH Construction

Corporation and went on to serve in numerous government-appointed positions, including the New York State Urban Development Corporation and the Metropolitan Transportation Authority, both of which he led as chairman. He also served as CEO of the Bowery Savings Bank. The author of *So Much to Do: A Full Life of Business, Politics, and Confronting Fiscal Crises* (Public Affairs 2014), Ravitch recently served as an adviser in the Detroit bankruptcy and also cochaired the State Budget Crisis Task Force with former Federal Reserve Board chairman Paul A. Volcker. He is a director of the Volcker Alliance, a nonprofit organization founded in 2013 to address the challenge of effective execution of public policy and help rebuild public trust in government.

Susan M. Wachter is the Sussman Professor and a professor of real estate and finance at the Wharton School of the University of Pennsylvania and cofounder and current codirector of the Penn Institute for Urban Research (Penn IUR). Wachter is a former assistant secretary for policy development and research at the U.S. Department of Housing and Urban Development and chairperson of Wharton's real estate department. She is the author of more than two hundred scholarly publications, including fifteen books. She frequently comments on national media and testifies to the U.S. Congress on housing policy.

References

American Cities Project. 2012. "The Local Squeeze: Falling Revenues and Growing Demand for Services Challenge Cities, Counties, and School Districts." Washington, D.C.: Pew Charitable Trusts.

Anderson, Michelle W. 2012. "Dissolving Cities." *Yale Law Journal* 121: 1364–446.

ASCE (American Society of Civil Engineers). 2013. *2013 Report Card for America's Infrastructure.* Reston, Va.: ASCE.

Bachman, Paul, Michael Head, and Frank Conte. 2013. "Public Pensions in Massachusetts: The True Cost." Beacon Hill Institute Policy Study, Suffolk University.

Becker-Medina, Erika, and Katheryn Brigham. 2013. "Public Pensions: State-Administered Defined Benefit Data Summary Report 2012." Washington, D.C.: U.S. Census Bureau.

Biggs, Andrew G. 2015. "The Public Pension Funding Trap." *Wall Street Journal,* May 31.

Brown, J., N. Liang, and S. Weisbenner. 2007. "Individual Account Investment Options and Portfolio Choice: Behavioral Lessons from 401(k) Plans." *Journal of Public Economics* 91(10): 1992–2013.

Chernick, Howard, Cordelia Reimers, and Jennifer Tennant. 2013. "Tax Structure and Revenue Instability: The Great Recession and the States." Paper presented at the Annual Conference of the National Tax Association, Providence, R.I.

Choi, J., D. Laibson, and B. Madrian. 2011. "$100 Bills on the Sidewalk: Suboptimal Investment in 401(k) Plans." *Review of Economics and Statistics* 43(3): 748–63.

Clarke, Katherine. 2015. "The South Bronx Sizzle: Once a Symbol of Urban Blight, the Formerly Burned Out Neighborhood Is Now a Major Draw for Investors." *New York Daily News,* April 8.

Costrell, Robert M. 2012. "GASB Won't Let Me—A False Objection to Public Pension Reform." Laura and John Arnold Foundation Policy Perspective.

Dadayan, Lucy, and Donald Boyd. 2013. "The Depth and Length of Cuts in State-Local Government Employment Is Unprecedented." Albany, N.Y.: The Nelson A. Rockefeller Institute of Government, University at Albany.

DiSalvo, Daniel. 2013. "Government Crowded Out: How Employee Compensation Costs Are Reshaping State and Local Government." New York: The Manhattan Institute.

Dubow, Rob. 2014. Presentation to Penn IUR Joint Fall Advisory Board and Executive Committee Meeting, November 11. Philadelphia.

Eucalitto, Cory. 2013. "Promises Made, Promises Broken—The Betrayal of Pensioners and Taxpayers." Charleston, S.C.: State Budget Solutions.

Fitzpatrick, Maria. 2015. "How Much Are Public School Teachers Willing to Pay for Their Retirement Benefits?" *American Economic Journal: Economic Policy*, forthcoming.

Fitzpatrick, IV, Thomas F., and Amy B. Monahan. 2014. "Who's Afraid of Good Governance? State Fiscal Crises, Public Pension Underfunding, and the Resistance to Governance Reform." *Florida Law Review* 66: 1317–73.

GAO (General Accountability Office). 1990. "States Help Communities in Fiscal Distress." GAO/HRD-90-69. Washington, D.C: Government Accountability Office.

Goldsmith, Stephen. 2010. "Red-Ink Tsunami: Why Old Ideas Can't Fix the New Government Perma-Crisis." New York: The Manhattan Institute, January 10.

Gómez, Rafael, and Pablo Hernández de Cos. 2008. "The Importance of Being Mature: The Effect of Demographic Maturation on Global Per Capita GNP." *Journal of Population Economics* 21: 589–608.

Harris, Benjamin. 2013. "Why State and Local Governments Are Hurting the Recovery." Washington, D.C.: Urban Institute–Brookings Institution Tax Policy Center.

Harris, Benjamin, and Yuri Shadunsky. 2013. "State and Local Governments in Economic Recoveries: This Recovery Is Different." Washington, D.C.: Urban Institute–Brookings Institution Tax Policy Center.

Kiewiet, D. Roderick. 2010. "The Day After Tomorrow: The Politics of Public Employee Retirement Benefits." *The California Journal of Politics and Policy* 2: 1–30.

Kiewiet, D. Roderick, and Mathew D. McCubbins. 2014. "State and Local Government Finance: The New Fiscal Ice Age." *Annual Review of Political Science* 17: 1–17.

Kogan, Vladimir, and Mathew McCubbins. 2010. "Changing Tracks? The Prospect for California Pension Reform." *California Journal of Politics and Policy* 2: 1–17.

LeDuff, Charles. 2013. *Detroit: An American Autopsy.* New York: Penguin Books.

Maddaus, Gene. 2013. "How Richard Riordan Blew $800,000 on a Failed Try at Pension Reform." *Los Angeles Weekly*, January 3.

Mincer, Jilian. 2012. "US Local Governments Take Budget Knife to Retiree Health Plans." Reuters, October 15.

Monahan, Amy. 2014. Presentation to Penn IUR Joint Fall Advisory Board and Executive Committee Meeting, November 11. Philadelphia.

———. 2015. "State Fiscal Constitutions and the Law and Politics of Public Pensions." *University of Illinois Law Review* 2015: 117–72.

Moretti, Enrico. 2012. *The New Geography of Jobs.* New York: Houghton Mifflin Harcourt Publishing Company.

Moringello, Juliet M. 2014. "Goals and Governance in Municipal Bankruptcy." *Washington and Lee Law Review* 71: 403–85.

National Conference of Commissioners on Uniform State Law. 1997. Uniform Management of Public Employee Retirement Systems Act. Available at http://www.uniformlaws.org/shared/docs/management_public_employee_retirement_systems/mpersa_final_97.pdf.

Novy-Marx, Robert, and Joshua Rauh. 2008. "The Intergenerational Transfer of Public Pension Promises." NBER Working Paper 14343. Cambridge, Mass.: National Bureau of Economic Research.

———. 2009. "The Liabilities and Risks of State-Sponsored Pension Plans." *Journal of Economic Perspectives* 23: 191–210.

———. 2010. "Pension Security Bonds: A New Plan to Address the Pension Crisis." *The Economists' Voice* 7(3).

———. 2011a. "Policy Options for State Pension Systems and Their Impact on Plan Liabilities." *Journal of Pension Economics and Finance* 10(2): 173–94.

———. 2011b. "Public Pension Liabilities: How Big Are They and What Are They Worth?" *Journal of Finance* 66(4): 1207–45.

———. 2011c. "The Crisis in Local Government Pensions in the United States." In *Growing Old: Paying for Retirement and Institutional Money Management after the Financial Crisis*, Robert Litan and Richard Herring, eds. Washington, D.C.: Brookings Institution Press.

———. 2012. "The Revenue Demands of Public Employee Pension Promises." Working Paper 18489. Cambridge, Mass.: The National Bureau of Economic Research.

———. 2014a. "Linking Benefits to Investment Performance in US Public Pension Systems." *Journal of Public Economics* 116: 47–61.

———. 2014b. "The Revenue Demands of Public Sector Pension Promises." *American Economic Journal: Economic Policy* 61(1): 193–229.

Oliff, Phil, Chris Mai, and Vincent Palacios. 2012. "States Continue to Feel Recession's Impact." Washington, D.C.: Center on Budget and Policy Priorities.

Passantino, George, and Adam Summers. 2005. "The Gathering Pension Storm: How Government Pension Plans Are Breaking the Bank and Strategies for Reform." Los Angeles: Reason Public Policy Institute.

Pension Benefit Guaranty Corporation. 2014. "PBGC Projections Report, FY 2013." Washington D.C.: Pension Benefit Guaranty Corporation.

Pew Center on the States. 2010. "The Trillion Dollar Gap: Underfunded State Retirement Systems and the Road to Reform." Washington, D.C.: The Pew Charitable Trusts.

———. 2013. "A Widening Gap in Cities: Shortfalls in Funding for Pensions and Retiree Health Care." Washington, D.C.: The Pew Charitable Trusts.

Poston, Ben, and Matt Stevens. 2015. "L.A's Aging Water Pipes; A $1-Billion Dilemma." *Los Angeles Times*, February 16.

Ravitch, Richard, and Paul A. Volcker. 2012a. *Report of the State Budget Crisis Task Force: New York Report.* New York: State Budget Crisis Task Force.

———. 2012b. *Report of the State Budget Crisis Task Force: Texas Report.* New York: State Budget Crisis Task Force.

Riordan, Richard J., and Tim Rutten. 2013. "A Plan to Avert the Pension Crisis." *The New York Times*, August 4.

Shnitser, Natalya. 2015. "Funding Discipline for U.S. Public Pension Plans: An Empirical Analysis of Institutional Design." *Iowa Law Review* 100: 663–714.

Snell, Ronald. 2012. "State Pension Reform, 2009–2011." Denver, Colo.: National Conference of State Legislatures.

Spiotto, James. 2012. "Financial Emergencies: Default and Bankruptcy." In *Oxford Handbook of State and Local Government Finance*, Robert D. Ebel and John E. Petersen, eds. Oxford Handbooks Online. Oxford, U.K.: Oxford University.

Splinter, David. 2011. "State Pension Contributions and Fiscal Stress." Houston, Tex.: Rice University.

Stanford Institutional Investors' Forum. 2007. Committee on Fund Governance Best Practice Principles. Stanford, Calif.

Tang, Ning, Olivia Mitchell, Gary Mottola, and Stephen Utkus. 2010. "The Efficiency of Sponsor and Participant Portfolio Choices in 401(k) Plans." *Journal of Public Economics* 94: 1073–85.

Tatum, Adam. 2013. "Case Study: Los Angeles's Pension Slide, 2003–2013." California Common Sense, February 28. Available at http://cacs.org/research/case-study-los-angeless-pension-slide-2003-2013/.

TRIP (National Transportation Research Group). 2013. "Bumpy Roads Ahead: America's Roughest Rides and Strategies to Make Our Roads Smoother." Washington, D.C: TRIP.

Van Binsbergen, Jules, Robert Novy-Marx, and Joshua Rauh. 2014. "Financial Valuation of PBGC Insurance with Market-Implied Default Probabilities." *Tax Policy and the Economy* 28: 133–54.

Vincent, Grayson, and Victoria Velkoff. 2010. "The Next Four Decades: The Older Population in the United States, 2010 to 2050." Current Population Report P25-1138. Washington, D.C.: U.S. Census Bureau.

Wachter, Susan, and Lei Ding. 2014. *Revitalizing American Cities.* Philadelphia: University of Pennsylvania Press.

Walsh, Mary Williams. 2013. "Pension Proposal Aims to Ease Burden on States and Cities." *New York Times*, July 9.

Walsh, Mary Williams, and Danny Hakim. 2012. "Public Pensions Faulted for Bets on Rosy Returns." *New York Times*, May 27.

World Bank. 2002. *Globalization, Growth and Poverty: Building an Inclusive World Economy*. Policy Research Reports. Washington, D.C., and New York: World Bank and Oxford University Press.